All Learning Is Self-Directed

How Organizations Can Support and Encourage Independent Learning

Daniel R. Tobin

ASTD

Ordering information: Books published by the American Society for
Training & Development can be ordered by calling 800.628.2783 or
703.683.8100, or via the Website at www.astd.org.

Library of Congress Catalog Card Number: 99-68260
ISBN: 1-56286-133-6

Contents

Preface   vii

Introduction: The Rising Demand for ISDL   1

A Growing Trend   1

The Impetus Behind ISDL   1

Empowerment or Abandonment   3

Today's Rapidly Changing World   7

1 Independent, Self-Directed Learning in the Workplace   9

The Four Stages of Learning   9

Self-Directed, Independent Learning   11

Using Independent, Self-Directed Learning Wisely   19

Learning Assignment   19

2 Creating a Positive Learning Environment   21

A Positive Learning Environment   22

Characteristics of a Positive Learning Environment   25

Independent Learning in a Company With a PLE   35

Learning Assignment   36

3 Making Employees Responsible for Their Own Learning   **39**

Identifying Your Own Learning Needs   40
Learning About the Company   42
Understanding Your Role in the Company   45
Understanding Career Paths Within the Company   47
Finding and Accessing Learning Resources   47
A Different Dimension of Learning: Learning From
    Other Employees   51
Helping Employees Learn to Learn   51
Applying Learning to the Employee's Work   53
The Role of Company Leaders and Managers   54
Learning Assignment   54

4 The Manager's Role in Independent Learning   **57**

The Manager's Role   58
Helping Employees Understand Their Roles in the
    Company   59
Helping Employees Develop Their Learning Plans   60
Helping Employees Identify and Access Learning
    Resources   62
Ensuring That Employee Learning is Applied to the Job   63
Other New Roles for Managers   64
Other Management Strategies   67
Preparing Managers for New Roles   68
Learning Assignment   70

5 Leadership's Role in Independent Learning   **73**

Communicating Company Goals   74
Modeling of Learning Activities by Top Managers   75
Encouraging Employee Learning   78
Learning Assignment   88

6 Redefining Corporate Training   **91**

Strategy 1: Arguing Against the Mandate   92
Strategy 2: Ignoring the Mandate   92
Strategy 3: Acceding to the Mandate   93
Strategy 4: Finding the Right Balance   95
New Roles for the Training Organization   103
The New Training Organization   110
Learning Assignment   111

7 Role of Technology-Based Training   **113**

Technology-Based Learning   114

Barriers to Technology-Based Training   126

The Role of Technology-Based Learning   131

Keeping Up With Innovations   131

Learning Assignment   132

8 Building and Using a Knowledge Network   **133**

Important Considerations for a Knowledge Network   138

The Knowledge Network as a Support to ISDL   146

The Training Organization's Role in the Knowledge
Network   148

Learning Assignment   150

**9 Growing and Sustaining an Independent
Learning Culture**   **153**

Getting ISDL Off the Ground   154

Helping Each Other Learn   163

Aligning Measurements and Rewards With ISDL   166

Growing and Managing an Independent Learning
Culture   169

Keeping the Organization Focused on Independent
Learning   170

Learning Assignment   171

10 Future of ISDL in the Workplace   **173**

Winning the Business of ChemGlobal   173

The Rest of the Story   182

Expanding the Story Beyond Bob and ProConsul   185

Learning Assignment   187

References   189

Additional Resources   191

About the Author   195

Preface

Several years ago, I received a call from a freelance writer who was working on an assignment from a major magazine in the HR field. The editor of the magazine had noted that more and more companies were moving toward "self-directed learning" and away from the traditional, instructor-led, classroom-instructional model. She asked me to think about the topic and to "come up with some type of challenging statement on the topic of self-directed learning."

When she called again a few days later, I was ready with a "challenging statement" for her article: "*All* learning is self-directed. Although the corporation or an instructional designer has designed the content of a training program to meet specific learning objectives, whether I am in a classroom, reading, or taking a computer-based training program, I, as the learner, decide what is important to me and, therefore, I choose what to learn." The learner may not have control over what is being *taught*, but the learner always has control over what is *learned*.

The trend toward self-directed learning, which was perceived several years ago by that publication and that writer, continues to grow. Sometimes that growth has proceeded wisely, and sometimes not.

What is needed is a rational approach to independent, self-directed learning—an approach that will help companies and their training groups take maximum advantage of the benefits of independent, self-directed learning (ISDL) while avoiding some of the common pitfalls that many companies have faced in trying to implement ISDL. This book is designed to fill that need. It is a learning resource for training and HRD professionals who are seeking guidance on how to make ISDL work within their companies.

I introduce the book by pointing out the reasons behind the movement toward ISDL and spelling out the responsibilities of the company and the employee in regard to training and learning. In chapter 1, I define terms and place ISDL into the framework of a four-stage learning model. To succeed in any organization, ISDL must be supported by a positive learning environment, which is defined and described in chapter 2.

Many companies have told employees that they must take responsibility for their own learning. Unfortunately, most of these companies fail to help employees identify their learning needs and find the necessary learning resources. In chapter 3, I discuss the true meaning of "making employees responsible for their own learning" and how companies must help employees if this strategy is to be successful. For employees to take on this responsibility, they are going to need help from their managers, as described in chapter 4. The company's leaders will also have to demonstrate the importance of employee learning—walking the talk—by demonstrating their own learning activities and taking steps necessary to create a positive learning environment, as described in chapter 5.

Switching emphasis from instructor-led training to ISDL should not portend the demise of the corporate training group. The corporate training group has a vital role to play in making ISDL successful, but this requires a redefinition of the corporate training group, as described in chapter 6.

One of the primary driving forces behind the movement to ISDL is the widespread availability of affordable technology-based training methods. In chapter 7, I offer my views of technology-based training (TBT), define the basic methods of TBT, and comment on how they are used and misused in today's corporations.

To reflect the ongoing convergence of training and knowledge management, in chapter 8 I describe a knowledge network that includes organizing content, managing connections, providing learning resources, and supplying learning tools in a comprehensive manner to facilitate and enable ISDL. Converting some of the company's training to ISDL is not a one-time effort—it's a cultural revolution. In chapter 9, I discuss what it takes to grow and sustain an independent learning culture.

Finally, in chapter 10, I provide an example of how ISDL might work in a company and discuss the future of ISDL in the workplace.

To help you extrapolate from this book to your own practice, I offer real-life stories collected from many different companies. I have also included many stories drawn from my own experiences as corporate training director for Wang Global, a multinational "network technology solutions and services" company headquartered in Billerica, Massachusetts, and throughout my career as both a training manager and consultant.

In addition, learning assignments appear at the end of each chapter to help you take this book into your own organizations and embark on your own ISDL programs. I designed some of the learning assignments to challenge traditional thinking and provide food for thought. Other learning assignments have charts to complete or questions to answer that can help you take real, practical steps toward bringing ISDL to your company.

It is my hope that you will find relevance and purpose in some of the ideas I offer in this book. But, as explained in the learning model in chapter 1, these ideas will only become your personal knowledge if you apply them to your work. After all, all learning is self-directed; what you learn is determined by you, not me.

Daniel R. Tobin
Framingham, Massachusetts
February 2000

Introduction: The Rising Demand for ISDL

A GROWING TREND

The proportion of corporate training done via instructor-led training is waning, and the proportion offered via various outside-the-classroom models is growing every year. Classroom-based training continues to be the training method of choice for about two-thirds of all corporate training today, but this is a smaller proportion than even a few years ago. I predict that independent, self-directed learning (ISDL) will reach a 50-50 split with instructor-led training within the next five to 10 years.

THE IMPETUS BEHIND ISDL

The movement to ISDL has been sparked by many different factors:

- Corporate downsizing and consolidation of corporate functions generate pressure to reduce corporate training budgets, including travel time and expense and the opportunity cost of time away from work for training.

- Corporate training directors are unable to show a positive return on the company's investments in training and development programs.
- Well-planned efforts take advantage of proliferating technology—personal computers, company networks, multimedia, and instructional-design tools—to create technology-based training and knowledge-management systems.

Corporate Downsizing

Despite the booming economy of the past few years, many companies have faced the necessity of downsizing: closing plants and business locations, laying off thousands of employees, reducing budgets for all functions, and examining which investments have yielded and will continue to yield the highest returns. Whether the downsizing is intended to avert the collapse of the company or to trim wasteful expenditures and put the company on a better financial footing for the future, many companies' training groups are among the first functions to be hit by the corporate axe and among the functions most devastated by the chopping—sometimes with good reason (Tobin 1997). When the corporate training function disappears, companies have little choice but to tell employees that they must take responsibility for their own learning.

Training's Poor Return-on-Investment

Over the past six years or so, I have received calls from a dozen or more corporate training directors all of whom have made the same basic request: "My CEO has just told me that I have to do a return-on-investment (ROI) study to justify my training group's budget. Can you help?" After examining several of these situations in great detail, I came to a singular conclusion: If you have waited until the CEO is demanding an ROI study to examine how you can demonstrate the value of training to the company's business goals, it is already too late to save the training group. The CEO has already decided to eliminate or drastically reduce the training function and is using the ROI study to justify the decision.

Many training directors, seeing the clouds on the horizon, aren't waiting for the storm to hit, but are moving quickly to reduce the size of their budgets and staffs. A primary vehicle for this cost reduction movement is technology-based training, which uses computers, networks, and other technologies to deliver training to employees, thereby reducing the need for instructors, classrooms, travel expenses, and employees taking time away from their jobs to attend training programs.

Unfortunately, many of these cost-cutting efforts have reduced costs but have done little or nothing to improve the company's business results (chapter 6). Of course, these cost reductions, even if neutral with respect to company benefits, may improve ROI, because if benefits are held constant, any reduction in costs will improve the benefit-cost ratio.

Well-Planned Movement to Appropriate Technologies

In a few cases (too few), forward-looking training directors have actually examined the trend toward ISDL, evaluated alternative approaches to delivering training and otherwise meeting employees' learning needs, and developed a comprehensive plan that incorporates the best of both traditional and more modern approaches to delivering training. This thoughtful, deliberate approach helps employees identify and satisfy their unique learning requirements and helps the company build and manage its inventory of knowledge and skills. This is the goal of this book—to provide you with the guidance you need so that you can become part of this well-planned movement to appropriate technologies.

EMPOWERMENT OR ABANDONMENT

Many companies are telling employees that they can no longer rely on the company to specify which courses are required or provide a full schedule of training classes. Some companies have told employees that they must take responsibility for their own learning, but have provided no guidance on how to determine learning needs and priorities, no help in finding and selecting learning resources, no coaching or reinforcement for the application of new skills and knowledge to the job. At many of these companies, this statement has been accompanied by the total elimination of the corporate training function, leaving employees totally on their own with regard to training and learning. Many of these companies have stated that this new approach is consistent with their movement to empower their employees, but simply telling employees that they are on their own, without providing any guidance or support isn't empowerment, it's abandonment.

The answer to this dilemma is a compromise: Employees must be responsible for their own learning, and companies must be responsible for supporting and guiding employees on their learning voyages. Is this a good thing or a bad thing? What does this trend mean in terms of:

- the amount of learning done by employees
- the amount of training done by companies
- the quality and effectiveness of training received by employees
- the role of the corporate-training group within the company?

Employee Learning

As training alternatives proliferate within and without their places of employment, many employees have become free agent learners. According to Shari Caudron (1999): "They're taking night classes on telecommunications and conflict management. They're enrolling in online master's degree programs. And long after the kids are asleep, they're learning how to design Webpages using store-bought software on their PCs. They read textbooks over breakfast, go to workshops during lunch, and turn on the TV during dinner—not to veg out, mind you, but to learn a new language or study microeconomics."

Certainly ISDL has an important role in any company's training strategy, but it should never be viewed as a way to eliminate all instructor-led training. Nor should the movement to ISDL be seen as a way to eliminate the need for a corporate training organization. Companies have a responsibility for helping employees to:

- identify their learning needs
- identify a range of alternative learning methods
- choose among those alternative methods
- apply new learning to their work.

Company Training

The sources for learning today are so varied and numerous that training groups have a difficult task in keeping up with them themselves, never mind advising employees about what options are available to them. So employees are going out and finding their own sources, leading to a trend toward disintermediation: The training group is no longer the major source or even the broker for much of the training being taken by the company's employees.

Employees learn of training opportunities from a potpourri of sources: the Internet, training announcements from professional associations, magazine subscriptions, and other media-based and direct-mail advertisements. From this selection, employees are making their own training and learning choices separate from anything that their companies' training groups offer.

Quality and Effectiveness of Training

The time I have spent with Wang Global has given me additional perspectives on ISDL as both a developer and a customer for the myriad ISDL tools and packaged programs that exist in today's market. Every week, I receive a dozen or more telephone calls, email messages, and mailings from companies peddling their latest tools, services, or packaged products.

Surprisingly (at least to me), many more suppliers of tools seem to be in the market today than producers of packaged programs. Every month, I read of at least several new suppliers of tools to create ISDL programs, many started with venture capital. In fact, Wall Street is now paying attention to the technology-based education market— something it didn't do even three years ago.

What surprises me most is the scarcity of companies creating packaged ISDL products for the corporate training market. Many suppliers target the computer technology education market, but it is more difficult to find ISDL programs on other subjects. What makes this so surprising is the low cost of entry into this market. For a few thousand dollars, including the cost of a personal computer with a writable CD-ROM drive and one of the many commercial CBT development programs, almost anyone can enter the ISDL business. Because of the low cost of entry, the field has yielded some terrible products and some very good products.

The Wang Global Example

In 1998, Wang Global signed a partnership agreement with Microsoft Corporation. Under the terms of this agreement, Wang Global pledged to create 2,000 Microsoft-certified systems engineers (MCSEs) and Microsoft-certified solution developers (MCSDs) over a three-year period. When I took the job as Wang Global's corporate training director and dean of Wang Global Virtual University (WGVU) several months later, plans were already well underway to use computer-based training (CBT) as the primary means of preparing employees for the requisite certification exams.

Throughout this book, I will refer back to Wang Global's Microsoft training programs as a primary example. As I write this book, the Microsoft training programs are still a work in progress. We are learning as we go; the Wang Global experience demonstrates some effective strategies for ISDL and some strategies that didn't work or needed improvement. I believe that the lessons we are learning will illustrate many of the major points that will be covered in this book.

The Role of Corporate Training

From my perspective, the singular purpose of any corporate training organization is to help the company and its employees achieve their business goals. The training organization must do this by facilitating individual and group learning keyed to employee and organizational business objectives. This means that the training group should help employees acquire the knowledge and skills they need to do their jobs. Some of this knowledge can come from training, but some of it can also come from learning from other employees' knowledge and experience, and this points to the whole field of knowledge management. This trend toward the convergence of training and knowledge management (Tobin 1997) is an important one in today's market.

Most knowledge-management initiatives are based on technology. But if knowledge management is to be truly successful in any company, the real issues that will determine the success or failure of knowledge-management initiatives are not technology issues, but learning issues. In this book, I argue that the corporate-training group must take a major role in any such initiative and that the building of a knowledge network is a prime ingredient in any company's ISDL strategy.

TODAY'S RAPIDLY CHANGING WORLD

Much of the movement toward ISDL can be attributed to today's rapidly changing business environment. Not only are the tools and technologies for learning being rapidly disseminated and new tools, technologies, and programs wildly proliferating, but this is also the age of mergers and acquisitions, leading to many challenges for companies and their training organizations.

My Rapidly Changing World

As I complete the writing of this book, my company, Wang Global, is being acquired by a similar company, Getronics. This will create a unique set of challenges for my training group:

Will multinational Getronics, headquartered in Amsterdam, Netherlands, want its corporate training function located in Billerica, Massachusetts?

A look at Getronics's Website reveals that it already offers many educational programs to its employees, and almost all of those programs are in an instructor-led format, whereas most of my group's programs are in an ISDL format. How will we resolve these inconsistencies in approach?

Only time will tell.

Chapter 1

Independent, Self-Directed Learning in the Workplace

Dozens of articles have appeared in the training literature in recent years on the movement toward ISDL. Some argue that the trend will benefit employees, and others say that it is the worst news employees have faced in decades. In this chapter, I will define ISDL and related terms. I'll start by describing my four-stage learning model and interpreting the model in terms of ISDL.

THE FOUR STAGES OF LEARNING

1. receive data

Every day, you are confronted with an endless maze of data (stage 1 in figure 1-1). Everything that you absorb through your eyes or ears—on paper or via telephone, email, Webpages, or through conversations you hold or overhear—is all data. Even if it were for some reason desirable, it would be impossible to absorb it all, much less make any sense of it. You must decide which pieces of this data are relevant to your job, your interests, and your learning needs.

This filtering of data to find that which is relevant and has purpose to us results in information (stage 2). Sometimes this filtering process

2. filter data for relevant information

Figure 1-1. The four stages of learning.

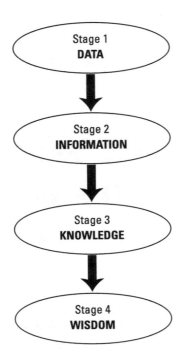

is done for you. For example, your manager decides what you need to know and sends only data that he or she deems appropriate. In other scenarios, the author of a book or training program decides to spend more time on one topic than on another, or the person of whom we ask a question tells us, "All you really need to know to get your job done is . . ." During classroom training at your company, at a public workshop, or in a college classroom, the instructor certainly is filtering data and deciding what is important for the students to learn.

Even when managers and instructors don't filter the data for you, you do it yourself. Few people read an entire newspaper or magazine, front page to back. Most decide what sections are of most interest, skim the titles of articles, and choose a few articles to read. Often, midway through a story or article, you decide that it doesn't have the information you hoped it would, and you stop reading it and move on to another article or story.

3. apply information so that it becomes knowledge

In stage 3, individuals apply the information from stage 2 to their work. Only after you have used information, tested it, seen how it works, and applied it to your work, can you say that you have mastered the information and that it has become part of your personal knowledge. It is at this stage that many corporate training programs fail, because the information imparted in many training programs never gets applied to people's work and, therefore, loses its value to the individual and to the company.

Part of the problem of applying information to work arises from the lack of a mechanism to support employees as they start to apply the information from training to work. Too often, instructors, managers, and co-workers are unavailable when a question arises. Rather than make an error or appear foolish, the employee abandons the new method in favor of the old: "It may not be as good as the new method, but I know how to do it, and I know it works."

4. Experience and experimentation result in gaining wisdom

To get to stage 4, wisdom, employees must continually apply their learning to their work, gaining experience and insight as to what works and what doesn't, how modifications to methods affect results, how different situations require slightly different solutions, and so forth. Through experience and experimentation, the employee gains the intuitive components of wisdom. Wisdom cannot be taught in a classroom or through any other type of instructional method. It is an internal process that takes time and experience. As I will discuss in later chapters, wisdom can be shared through dialogue and demonstration.

In the next section, I will show how this model relates to ISDL.

SELF-DIRECTED, INDEPENDENT LEARNING

What do we mean by self-directed, independent learning? Can learning be self-directed, but not independent? Independent, but not self-directed? Neither independent nor self-directed? Why is this of interest? Let's examine each of the terms in the context of the workplace.

Independent Learning

Independent learning, in the context of the workplace, is learning that takes place apart from other people. When you learn independently, you are not part of a class or a workgroup or a team. You learn in isolation. Of course, most learning is dependent on other people: a teacher; the writer of a book, article, or training program; or a colleague who answers a question. In the context of the workplace, independent learning refers to learning that takes place apart from formal, organized training programs. There are no instructors, no classmates, no designated day and time to show up for training. It's just you and your learning materials.

It is up to you to sort through the masses of data that are available on any given subject to find the information you need—the data that is relevant to your work, that satisfies your purpose in undertaking the learning. In most cases, this is not truly independent learning. When you choose a textbook or a self-paced learning program (on paper or computer-based), you have already given up some of your independence, because you have relied on the author of those materials to decide for you what is most important for you to learn.

The only truly independent learning is that which comes from experimentation and discovery. When Thomas Edison undertook his voyage of discovery to find a material for light-bulb filaments, he experimented with thousands of different materials before hitting upon tungsten. This was as close to independent learning as I believe that one can get. But even Edison had to rely upon the previous work of others to identify the thousands of materials he would test.

If you try out a new software program before opening the manual or if you attempt different solutions to a problem, you are learning what works and what doesn't. This is also a type of independent learning. Whether this type of learning is efficient doesn't really matter to you as long as the learning takes place and the job gets done.

Self-Directed Learning

Self-directed learning implies that you are deciding for yourself what you will learn and how you will learn it. You are directing your own learning activities. You are in charge. No one tells you what you must learn or decides which method is the best one for you to use. No one dictates when and where you must be in class. No one decides what is important for you to learn or what is not important.

I believe that all learning is self-directed. No matter what is taught in a classroom, no matter what the intention of a book's author, no matter how complete a computer-based training program may be, it is the individual learner who decides what is relevant to the job or the situation, what is important to him or her, and, therefore, what will be learned and retained. If the learning is dependent on an instructor or if it is totally independent of others, the individual's learning is always self-directed. Of course, when you take a course that includes a final examination, there may be learning requirements imposed on you related to passing the course, but the real learning— what you will retain and use after the class is completed—is determined by you.

Categorizing Learning Types

Although there is a definite trend in the corporate world toward ISDL, not all learning is or should be in this category. Let's look at the four possible categories of learning using these two definitions and see where some common types of learning might fall in terms of dependent versus independent and self-directed versus other-directed learning. The criteria we will use in each of the four quadrants of table 1-1 are:

- Who determines what must be learned?
- Who selects learning methods, materials, and schedules?
- Who measures the results of the learning activities?

In quadrant I, self-directed, dependent learning, it is the employee who decides what he or she must learn. At the same time, the employee is then dependent on the company or other people and organizations to provide learning methods, materials, and schedules. For example, the company may provide a catalog of company-sponsored training programs, both classroom-based and self-paced, or a learning center with a library of self-study materials. Similarly, a local college or other professional training providers may supply catalogs and

Table 1-1. Four types of learning.

	OTHER-DIRECTED	SELF-DIRECTED
INDEPENDENT	**Quadrant III** Learning topics, methods, and materials selected by the company. Employee may have some choice as to method and schedule, but must prove mastery of the learning content.	**Quadrant IV** Learning topics, methods, materials, and schedule selected by the employee. Employee is solely responsible for what is learned.
DEPENDENT	**Quadrant II** Learning topics, methods, materials, and schedule selected by the company, which also provides instruction. Employee is tested at end of program to prove mastery of the learning content.	**Quadrant I** Learning topics selected by the employee, but the employee is dependent on the company or another source for determining learning methods, materials, and schedules.

schedules of courses. So, although the employees determine their own learning needs, they must rely on others to point them to the available learning resources to meet those learning needs.

This is a common situation in many companies. Suppose that you wish to improve your presentation skills. In looking for learning resources, you may find that your company offers presentation-skills workshops or provides relevant audio- or videotapes in the corporate learning center. Perhaps you will find that local colleges have weekend workshops on presentation skills or that your local library has a book on the subject.

In quadrant II—other-directed, dependent learning—the company determines for its employees both their learning requirements and the methods, materials, and schedules for related learning activities. The company mandates the employee's learning activities.

Other-directed, dependent learning often involves topics that are mandated by legal authorities or by company policy, as with safety training. Safety training may be mandated by a federal or state regulatory agency or by the company's insurance company. The company determines what the content of the training will be, how instruction will take place, and each employee's schedule for training. The company may also require some form of testing that measures employees' mastery of the content. Employees have no choice on what they will learn, how they will learn it, or when they will take training.

In quadrant III—other-directed, independent learning—the company determines what employees must learn but then leaves it to the employees to determine how they may best acquire that learning. For example, a company may introduce a new email system. By replacing the old system, if one existed, with the new system, the company doesn't give the employee any choice but to learn to use the new system. Perhaps the company schedules a series of training sessions for employees, but attendance is not mandatory. At the same time, the company may make available a set of other learning resources, such as

---

Making Other-Directed, Dependent Learning More Palatable

For the initial hospital-wide safety CBT, the education department at South Jersey Hospital had a contest to name the seven computer terminals that would be used. These terminals would be placed on carts to be rolled from department to department in each of our four facilities. The contest was announced by placing a tent card on each cafeteria table and in the biweekly employee newsletter. We placed tables with ballots and contest boxes at the entrance to each cafeteria with large notices explaining the new program and how the contest worked. Employees were given two weeks to submit entries. Education-department staff selected the winner who dubbed the system the "Brainy Bunch" and each terminal "Marsha Brainy," "Greg Brainy," and so forth. The winner was rewarded with a gift certificate to a very nice local restaurant.

When we initiated the CBT program about two weeks after the close of the contest, distinctive name labels were made for each computer. This contest created a lot of interest and discussion without a heavy, authoritarian tone: "You have to do your mandatory training this new way now!" The response to the program was generally positive, although many complained about how long it takes to complete the lessons since each screen is held for a specified time without regard to the user's prior knowledge or comprehension ability.*

---

user manuals and computer-based training programs, to help employees learn to use the new system. Employees may choose one of these methods or may simply ask a colleague who has already learned the system to show them the ropes. Although there are no mastery tests, it is made clear to all employees that they must learn the material.

In quadrant IV—self-directed, independent learning—employees are on their own to determine what they want to learn or must learn and how best to accomplish that learning. The company provides no guidance on topics, methods, or learning resources and sets no deadlines for completing the employee-selected learning activities. For example, an employee who has been given some project management responsibilities may decide that to be effective in this new role he or she should learn about project management methods and tools. The employee then must identify what he or she needs to learn and seek available learning resources, both within and without the company. The employee then selects the best learning resources, according to learning preferences, sets up a schedule for completing the selected learning activities, and then determines how to apply the learning at work. Only the employee measures the learning; no tests are administered. The company manager is not concerned with the employee's learning plan, only job performance.

Choosing the Category of Learning

How do you determine into which of the four quadrants a particular learning need falls? Two basic questions can help you place any given topic into one of the four quadrants.

- *Is there a clear reason why all company employees, or a specific subset of employees, must master a new set of skills or body of knowledge?* If there is a clear mandate, such as from legal or regulatory requirements, the learning should fall into the other-directed (or company-directed) column (quadrants II and III). If no clear mandate exists, employees should be made aware of the potential learning need in this area of skill or knowledge, but should decide for themselves or with their managers whether to pursue learning in this area.

- *Is there a clear reason why the company should provide specific training to employees for these skills or body of knowledge?* The company might decide that it must provide training to all employees for several reasons. As discussed earlier, training may be mandated by a regulatory agency. Perhaps the company has to meet a deadline for completion of training to satisfy a customer or contractual requirement. The company, facing the need to train a large number of employees, may decide that creating its own training program is the most cost-effective way of reaching the training goal. Under these circumstances, it is sometimes wise to make the employee dependent on the company for the training. Otherwise, allowing independent choice of learning methods and schedules may be wiser.

The key is flexibility: Allow employees to determine their own learning needs, methods, and schedules insofar as possible, and, at the same time, ensure that the company's business goals are being met.

Creating Microsoft-Certified Personnel at Wang Global

Wang Global faced the challenge of creating 2,000 MCSEs and MCSDs in a mere three years. The learning that a Wang Global employee had to undertake to become an MCSE or MSCD was mandated by Microsoft's certification requirements—the training was other-directed. At the same time, dozens of alternative learning methods and materials were available in the marketplace, all from Microsoft-certified training partners and, therefore, any or all could be used to satisfy Microsoft's requirements.

Although the partnership agreement with Microsoft set deadlines for completion of training and certification, it did not specify training methods or materials for the training. One vital question we faced in my first weeks with the company was: Should Wang Global mandate training methods and materials for its employees or let employees choose their own methods and materials?

(continued on next page)

Creating Microsoft-Certified Personnel at Wang Global *(continued)*

We decided to specify the training methods (CBT with online mentoring services) and materials (we selected the suppliers for the CBT programs, the online mentoring service, and additional study materials we provided to student-employees). We based the decisions primarily on the economics of the situation: By purchasing these services and materials in large quantities, we could negotiate substantial discounts instead of having each employee seek his or her own training services and materials.

We found that we had to build in flexibility to accommodate some special cases. For example, some employees had already embarked on their own learning programs before the corporate program was announced. Some employees were near completion of the requirements at a local college or university, or with a particular training vendor. In many of those cases, it made sense to allow the employee to complete the program he had already started. In other cases, we allowed the employee to complete the course or certification examination on which he was currently working before requiring him to switch over to the new, corporate-mandated methods and materials.

In a few cases, we had a deadline to get a group of students through the training and certification process faster than the company-standard approach in order to fulfill a customer requirement. To meet this need, the company built or bought from other suppliers special, fast-track training methods and materials.

Although no employees stated that they couldn't learn effectively from the methods being prescribed by the company, we were prepared to respond to employees' varying learning styles and needs by bringing in other learning methods and materials as the need arose.

I don't believe that any company can succeed in meeting its business goals by simply eliminating the corporate training function and telling employees that they must take responsibility for their own learning. To me, this isn't empowerment, as some companies claim, but abandonment.

USING INDEPENDENT, SELF-DIRECTED LEARNING WISELY

How a company and its employees learn and how they apply their individual and collective learning to their work to help achieve personal, group, and corporate goals is the single most important factor in any company's future success. Independent, self-directed learning has an important role to play in the business environment of today and tomorrow. Indeed, it occupies an even more important role than traditional training and development groups have played in the corporate environment over the past several decades.

To succeed with this new approach, companies are going to have to change. They will have to change the way they think about training and learning, how managers and leaders interact with employees about learning requirements and the application of learning to the job, how to determine learning needs, and how to identify and access learning resources throughout the company. They will have to change their thinking about the role of the corporate training function in the company and how it is organized and run. It all starts with building a positive learning environment, the subject of my next chapter.

LEARNING ASSIGNMENT

Let's start applying the material from this book to your job. This chapter contained a lot of data, and I hope that at least some of it is relevant to your job. If so, this data has become information (stage 2 of learning). The learning assignments at the end of each chapter are designed to help you apply that information to your work, thus helping you make the transition from information to knowledge (stage 3). Your first learning assignment is this:

1. Think about your last learning activity—something you learned at or away from work, from a training class, a college course, a professional conference, a trade show, a book or article, or from a conversation you had over lunch with a colleague. Write a brief summary of that learning activity.

2. Place this learning activity into the appropriate quadrant in the matrix below.

3. If the learning activity was important to your job or to your organization, into which quadrant should the learning activity have fallen?

4. If the quadrant placements for questions 2 and 3 are different, ask yourself these questions:
   - How could you get it moved from where it was to where it should be?
   - Who would make the decision?
   - How could you, as an individual employee, or as a manager or training or HR professional, influence that decision?

	OTHER-DIRECTED	SELF-DIRECTED
INDEPENDENT	**Quadrant III** Independent, Other-Directed Learning	**Quadrant IV** Independent, Self-Directed Learning
DEPENDENT	**Quadrant II** Dependent, Other-Directed Learning	**Quadrant I** Dependent, Self-Directed Learning

ENDNOTE

* Provided by and printed by permission from Florence Mori and Cindi Calebrese, staff development coordinators, South Jersey Hospital.

All Learning Is Self-Directed

Chapter 2

Creating a Positive Learning Environment

O ften, when I give a speech or seminar, I ask the audience one or both of these questions:

- How would you feel if your CEO walked into your office and found you reading a book?

- How would your manager respond to this request: "I'd like to spend one morning a month at the local university library reading the latest industry journals and magazines to try to find some new ideas to help us improve our operations"?

In response to the first question, most people say that they would be embarrassed that they "weren't working." I tell them that if their company has a positive learning environment, learning, including reading a book at your desk, would be just as legitimate and important to their jobs as other activities (assuming that the book is job-related and not a romance novel).

In response to the second question, most audience members say that their manager's answer would probably be: "That's a great idea, but why don't you do it on your own time. We're paying you to work, not to spend time at the library." Again, I make the point that if the company has a positive learning environment, the search for new ideas to improve individual, group, and overall company performance is viewed as a critical part of everyone's job.

Although both of these questions deal with reading, people learn in many other ways, as discussed throughout this book, and all of those methods should be an integral part of the company's learning environment. So, what do I mean by a positive learning environment? How can you tell if your company has such an environment? How can you build a positive learning environment in your company? Let's start off with a basic definition and then move on to the characteristics of a positive learning environment.

A POSITIVE LEARNING ENVIRONMENT

A positive learning environment (PLE) encourages, even demands, that every employee at every level be in a continuous learning mode, constantly searching for new ideas, trying new methods, sharing ideas and learning with others, and learning from others, to find new and better ways to achieve individual, group, and organizational business goals.

When I say "encourages, even demands," I mean that the organization doesn't just wait for someone to come along with a better idea. A PLE is one where leaders, managers, and employees at all levels are constantly on the watch for ways to improve business results. Every idea, no matter what the source, is evaluated to determine if it is worth implementing or at least worth more investigation. The organization's leaders and managers encourage their employees to constantly learn and to search for new ways to improve their own and the organization's business performance.

Many companies put nice-sounding platitudes in their company philosophies or in their annual reports: "Our employees and their knowledge are the company's most important asset, and we do everything we can to ensure that these assets are nurtured and grown." But then the companies do nothing to implement the philosophical statement or act in ways that actually discourage employee learning. How do companies hinder learning? The following comments, which are too often heard in meetings, can stifle learning and even the desire to learn:

- That's a dumb idea!
- Who asked you?
- What do you know about it? Leave it to people who know what they're talking about.
- We tried that a few years ago at one of our plants. It doesn't work.
- It may have worked at your former company, but we're different.
- We've had a procedure for that in place for the past five years, and it works. If it ain't broke, don't fix it.
- We're paying you to get your job done, not to think about things that aren't your responsibility.

By "every employee at every level," I mean just that—learning starts in the office of the chairman and CEO and extends to every employee in the organization. For a manager at any level to say "my employees have a lot to learn," and at the same time deny his or her own learning needs, makes it clear that learning is not valued. Every person, at every level, must be in a continuous learning mode.

By "continuous learning mode," I mean that learning should be an important part of every employee's job, with learning taking place every day. Many companies can point to a company policy that guarantees every employee will receive 40 hours (or more) of training every year as proof that they have a PLE. But 40, 80, or even 120 hours of formal training a year does not mean that an employee is in a continuous learning mode. Learning encompasses much more than formal classroom training and must be an integral part of every employee's job description if a company wants to have a positive learning environment.

Employees who are in a continuous learning mode are "constantly searching for new ideas, trying new methods, sharing ideas and learning with others, and learning from others." These are all forms of learning. Some of it comes from formal classroom instruction. Other parts come from formal, self-directed, and independent learning activities, such as reading, taking CBT or other media-based instruction, or

What If . . . ?

What if every manager in your organization from the CEO on down started every staff meeting with this question: "What have we learned since our last meeting that we can use to improve our operations and our results?" Starting every meeting with this question would make it clear to every employee at every level of the organization that learning—seeking new ways to improve the organization's operations and enhance individual, group, and companywide results—is the top-priority agenda item for everyone in the organization. If my manager repeatedly asked the same question, I would be certain that I had answers to give. I would make certain that I was indeed learning every day and trying to find new and better ways of doing my job.

other activities that we generally deem to be in the category of learning and self-study. But most true learning comes not from studying, but from applying new ideas to your work, finding out what works and what doesn't, and searching for even minor improvements in results. And even more learning takes place when employees share their learning with others and, in turn, learn from others to help them improve their own results.

In many factory environments, starting with the famed Toyota manufacturing system, major improvements in productivity come not from major reworking of the overall system of manufacture, but from small, incremental improvements to every aspect of the manufacturing operation. When you see a factory that boasts eight to 10 percent annual improvements in productivity over a number of years, you can be certain that these arise from the small learning steps that define a continuous improvement environment. You can't have continuous improvement without continuous learning.

Finally, my definition of a PLE concludes with the phrase: "to find new and better ways of achieving individual, group, and organizational business results." Unless learning activities are focused on improving business results, they probably won't. My guiding principle as a training professional, as a consultant, and as an author has always been that all learning activities that I sponsor must be directly linked to a specific business need. Too often, in my experience and observations, training activities don't have this tie-in to the organization's business goals and, as a result, when company leaders ask the training group for an ROI justification for the training budget, a positive calculation will almost never result. When company leaders see that all learning is tied directly to the company's business goals, they will never ask for a ROI study, for they will see the results every day in every part of the company.

CHARACTERISTICS OF A POSITIVE LEARNING ENVIRONMENT

Often, when I present the above definition of a PLE, audience members ask me how they would know a PLE if they saw one or how they can tell if their company has a PLE. For this purpose, it will be useful to list some of the characteristics of a PLE. This section will be primarily descriptive of these characteristics. In later chapters, I will provide more pointers on how to build a PLE, including step-by-step instructions for many of the items listed below.

Gathering a List of PLE Characteristics

To test the pulse of the profession, I surveyed the members of TRDEV-L, a moderated listserv discussion group hosted by Pennsylvania State University (1999). This listserv has more than 5,000 members in the training and development field around the world. I received more than two dozen responses to my query: "How would you define the characteristics of a positive learning environment?"

The responses varied widely, but all seemed focused on something more than the current situation in their organizations. For example, one person responded: "Having a real training group in the company would be a real positive step." Another person asked: "What percentage of your employees have individual development plans? Of those, how many actually use them?" Another member of the listserv discussion forum suggested that an indication of a PLE would be managers who say: "Don't worry, while you're attending that training session, I've arranged for someone to cover your workload." The most comprehensive list of PLE characteristics came from Mike Kunkle, vice president of professional services at PlanSoft Corporation. To develop table 2-1, I have supplemented his list with 15 items of my own. Following the table are in-depth discussions of these characteristics. Note that this list is not meant to be exhaustive; in fact, the learning assignment for this chapter will ask you to add other indicators of a PLE that come from your own experience.

Table 2-1. Thirty ways to know you are working in a positive learning environment.

1. Ideas are openly solicited from employees at all levels, formally and informally.
2. Messengers are welcomed, not shot.
3. Mistakes are viewed as education.
4. Company pays for association dues and work-related subscriptions.
5. Censorship and negative politics are at a minimum or nonexistent.
6. Employees can freely challenge ideas presented by management, without fear of retribution.
7. Focus-group-like meetings are encouraged.
8. Brainstorming is common.
9. On-the-job training is used.
10. Training is encouraged where appropriate.
11. Supervisors learn what their subordinates are learning in training, and reinforce that learning.
12. Coaching is common.
13. Learning is a process, not an event.
14. 360-degree surveys are common.
15. The performance appraisal process is not dreaded and is linked to employee learning and growth.
16. Cross-functional teamwork is common.
17. Task forces draw employees from all levels, geographies, and business units.
18. Every employee is able to give a company overview presentation.
19. Employees are encouraged to enlarge their jobs and to learn about the jobs of their internal and external customers and suppliers.
20. Career paths within the company extend beyond functional, business unit, and geographic boundaries.
21. Employees are encouraged to talk with one another to exchange ideas and solve problems.

Table 2-1. Thirty ways to know you are working in a positive learning environment. *(continued)*

22. The company publishes learning guides for employees in all functions at all levels.
23. The company provides access to the company library and Internet resources.
24. Job shadowing is encouraged.
25. Brown-bag seminars are given regularly.
26. Executives spend time talking with, and listening to, employees.
27. Mentoring programs exist at all levels.
28. Employees are encouraged and rewarded for outside work in their professions.
29. Employees are constantly on the prowl for best, or better, practices.
30. Employees look forward to meetings.

Source: Items 1–15 were provided by and reprinted with permission of Mike Kunkle, vice president of professional services, PlanSoft Corporation.

A Closer Look at PLE Characteristics

The list of PLE indicators merits further attention. In the following paragraphs, I expand upon Mike Kunkle's ideas (items 1–15) and my own.

1. Ideas are openly solicited from employees at all levels, formally and informally. Only when everyone's ideas are valued and sought can you say that you have a PLE. For example, in some companies, the CEO holds quarterly all-employee meetings, which start at a given time, but don't end until every question is asked and answered. General Electric Corporation's famed "workout" sessions have senior corporate executives meet with first-level employees to hear their ideas and make immediate commitments to those ideas that have merit. Sears, Roebuck and Company's corporate executives spend time every week in their stores soliciting ideas from employees about what is working and what isn't and gathering their ideas for improvements.

2. Messengers are welcomed, not shot. No situation can be improved unless there is recognition that a problem exists. In companies where the messengers are shot, not much learning takes place, because employees know that their managers are not interested in hearing their ideas. In a PLE, employees are encouraged to point out problems and, even more important, to make recommendations on how the problems can be solved.

3. Mistakes are viewed as education. One often-heard story involves a fast-track young executive who one day made a mistake that cost his large, multinational company a million dollars. Upon arriving at work the next morning, the young executive was called to the office of a senior officer of the company. The officer asked for an explanation of what happened. After stammering out his explanation, the young executive nervously queried: "You're going to fire me, aren't you?" "Why would I want to do that?" replied the officer. "I just spent a million dollars on your education."

4. Company pays for association dues and work-related subscriptions. By attending local and national professional association meetings and by reading professional and industry publications, employees expand their horizons beyond their own jobs, their own company, and their own industry. They can learn from the experiences of others,

---

Paying for Mistakes

At one company, if employees follow a logical sequence of steps and arrive at a poor conclusion or make an error, managers can offer them $50 to write up the error and publicize it to other employees. When this plan was first suggested, employees looked askance at it: "Why should I humiliate myself?" But, the plan made sense for employees and for the company. If one employee followed a logical course of action that led to an error, other people could just as easily follow the same course, leading to more of the same errors. By publicizing the errors, the company could help other employees avoid making the same error—well worth the $50 investment. And employees, rather than being humiliated, often receive thanks from other employees: "I almost made the same mistake. You saved me a lot of time and grief by publishing your experience. Thanks for letting me learn from you."

---

using these meetings and journals to do informal benchmarking and to gather new ideas to improve their own, their group's, and the company's work.

5. Censorship and negative politics are at a minimum or nonexistent. In a PLE, great ideas come from all levels, all teams, all business units, all geographies. Each idea is valued on its merit rather than on the level and position of its source. When you see a company that has a formal system for receiving suggestions but few suggestions are made, it is a sign that employees believe that management won't listen to their suggestions. When suggestion systems first start, employees are usually enthusiastic, but that enthusiasm wanes quickly if management rejects most of the suggestions made. An active suggestion system is one sign of a PLE.

6. Employees can freely challenge ideas presented by management, without fear of retribution. Ideas from any and all levels are open to discussion in a PLE. Few, if any, ideas are perfect, but almost all can be improved when an atmosphere of open discussion prevails, with everyone's goal being to find the best way of proceeding.

7. Focus-group-like meetings are encouraged. This is just one of many ways to help people express their ideas and get feedback on those ideas. These meetings, as well as companywide meetings and discussions on the company's intranet, bring people's ideas to the surface and provide a forum for feedback.

8. Brainstorming is common. This type of discussion, as is true for focus groups, is common, frequent, and involves all or most employees, drawing ideas from many sources in a freewheeling atmosphere, and is another indicator of a company with a PLE.

9. On-the-job training is used. On-the-job training was once the province of the factory floor, where new employees were shown how to do their jobs and then expected to do them flawlessly. But on-the-job training is a valuable member of the learning toolbox that should be available to all employees at all levels in all parts of the business.

10. Training is encouraged where appropriate. With the movement to independent, self-directed learning, some companies have all but abandoned traditional, classroom-based, live instruction. This is a mistake because sometimes the only effective method of training involves an instructor and a classroom.

11. Supervisors learn what their subordinates are learning in training, and reinforce that learning. Too often, when employees learn something new, whether in a classroom, from a self-study program, or by any other means, and then try to implement that learning on the job, they are stifled the first time that they encounter problems. There's no one to ask for help. The supervisor is unfamiliar with the learning, the instructor is teaching another class, the author of the book is unavailable, and so forth. In these cases, it often happens that the employees abandon the new methods in favor of the old, for fear of getting poor job evaluations or being embarrassed: "The old way may not be the best, but I know it works." When supervisors take and master the training first, employees are much more likely to integrate the new knowledge or skills successfully into their jobs, because the supervisors can answer questions and reinforce the employees' application of the learning.

12. Coaching is common. Coaching is the process of helping an employee master newly acquired skills and knowledge and apply them correctly to the job. A coach can be the employee's supervisor, a coworker, another member of the employee's team, or anyone else who has the required knowledge and skills. Learning doesn't stop when an employee finishes a course or completes a self-study assignment, but extends onto the job itself. It is there that coaching is invaluable.

13. Learning is a process, not an event. In a positive learning environment, learning is a continuous process, not something that happens one or two weeks a year.

14. 360-degree surveys are common. For everyone from the CEO down through the rest of the company, the 360-degree survey can be an important tool for discovering areas of learning needs and in evaluating how employee learning has affected individual, group, and company business results.

15. The performance appraisal process is not dreaded and is linked to employee learning and growth. Whether using 360-degree surveys or other methods, employee appraisal must be viewed as a guide for future learning. My recommended method of employee appraisal ties evaluations directly to employee-learning contracts (chapter 4).

16. Cross-functional teamwork is common. I always refer to teams as learning teams. From my point of view, the only reason why any company should ever put together a team is so that team members can learn from each other or together learn something new. If neither of these conditions is present, I don't believe that there is any reason to start a team. Cross-functional teaming allows employees to learn more about the company's overall business processes, removes their functional blinders, and enables team members to better contribute to the achievement of overall, organization-wide goals. Widespread use of cross-functional learning teams is one indicator of a PLE.

17. Task forces draw employees from all levels, geographies, and business units. Leadership, in any area of the company, draws on employees from all levels, business units, and geographies. Leadership is not solely the province of top management but comes from all parts of the company. When assembling a task force, whether to lead the United Way campaign, plan a new product line, or revamp the company's job classification and compensation system, find the right people for the job. Don't select members according to position or level.

18. Every employee is able to give a company overview presentation. Most companies have a standard presentation that provides an overview of the company's business, markets, customers, goals, and vision for the future. The presentation is often developed by the corporate communications group and is made available to the company's top officers and official spokespeople. Very often, rank-and-file employees have never seen the presentation. I believe that in a company with a PLE, not only would every employee be familiar with the presentation, but also every employee would be able to give it. This is not a matter of giving every employee a course on presentation skills, but rather ensuring that every employee understands the company's business well enough to give the presentation. It also would mean that every employee identified so well with the company's business and his or her role in the company that he or she would feel comfortable being identified as a company spokesperson. Think about it. Would you want to work for such a company? I would.

19. Employees are encouraged to enlarge their jobs, to learn about the jobs of their internal and external customers and suppliers. In a company with a PLE, employees are encouraged to develop their understanding of the context of the their jobs. While they focus on the skills and knowledge they need to do their own jobs, they also learn how their work fits into the larger context of the business by learning more about the jobs of their customers and suppliers, whether they are inside or outside the actual company. Sometimes this is referred to as "one-up, one-down" learning—learning about the jobs above and below your own on the company's economic-value chain.

20. Career paths within the company extend beyond functional, business unit, and geographical boundaries. Whether through formal succession planning (typically done by the company), employee-development planning (done by managers), or individual initiative, opportunities for growth include horizontal movement across boundaries, as well as vertical moves up the career ladder. This is especially important in today's business environment, which is typified by relatively flat organizational hierarchies with fewer rungs on career ladders and more people vying for fewer vertical movement opportunities.

21. Employees are encouraged to talk with one another to exchange ideas and solve problems. This indicator receives a lot of lip service, but in a PLE, these types of discussions are not only encouraged but enabled by the company. Many companies have built soundproof conference rooms in the middle of noisy factories to enable employees to meet together to discuss ideas for improvement. Many other companies have built wide-ranging discussion forums on the company's intranet to encourage the sharing and discussion of ideas. These are both indicators of a PLE.

22. The company publishes learning guides for employees in all functions at all levels. These learning guides, built on the competencies identified for various jobs within the company, help employees identify the areas in which they need development and then point employees to learning resources within and without the company. The Dow Chemical Company has made some major strides in this area.

23. The company provides access to the company library and Internet resources. In companies with a PLE, employees are given the tools to find the information they need from a company library or from massive resources available on the Internet. These companies are not worried about their employees wasting time searching for inappropriate material on the Internet but trust employees to use the resources to enable them to improve their own and the company's performance. It's not a matter of "Do it on your own time," but of "What can you find that can help us all work smarter?"

24. Job shadowing is encouraged. At travel giant Rosenbluth International, any employee wanting to learn about another part of the company or about the work of another person can ask to work in a different department or to shadow that person for a day. The purpose may be general education about the company's business or the exploration of a new career path. Everyone is eligible to do this with any other company employee, including CEO Hal Rosenbluth. One Rosenbluth International employee told me that she had signed up to shadow Hal on a given day. The day before, he came to her and said that he had to go to Mexico for the day. Rather than postpone the shadowing, he gave her a ticket and she went with him.*

25. Brown-bag seminars are given regularly. In some companies, employees are encouraged to share their knowledge and skills with others, whether they relate to the job or not. For example, in one company, employees are given a small payment to conduct a brown-bag (bring your lunch) seminar on any topic they believe would be of interest to other employees. Topics can span a wide range: ideas gathered at a recently attended conference, shortcuts the employee discovered in using the company's database system, or even gardening tips. Although the last topic may seem to be beyond the company's realm of responsibility for employee learning, it helps build an environment in the company where people get to know each other and openly share their knowledge, skills, and ideas in any area—a true characteristic of a PLE.

26. Executives spend time talking with, and listening to, employees. In some companies, executives regularly visit the employee cafeteria and sit down at random with employees to hear from the grassroots level how things are going. They may ask questions about specific programs, a new piece of machinery, a procedure recently introduced in the company, or they may just listen to whatever the employees want to talk about. The extent to which executives really listen and then act on what they have heard can say much about the learning environment in the company. In companies without a PLE, executives often have their own dining room and wouldn't even think about going to the company cafeteria to mix with rank-and-file employees.

27. Mentoring programs exist at all levels. A mentor acts as a counselor, gives advice on career paths and development opportunities, and provides an overview of what it takes to become a leader in the company. Typically, a mentor is a senior manager, at least two levels above the employee in the organization. The mentor must have broader experience in the company and the ability to place the employee into assignments that will help with the employee's development. A critical element in the mentoring relationship is mutual respect between the employee and the mentor. For example, the publisher of one of my books told me that he was assigned a mentor when he first joined a large publishing company. "Once a month, I had lunch with my mentor, a senior vice president in the company. I learned more about the publishing industry and how the company really worked at those lunches than I could have in years if I had to discover all of it myself." Too often, mentoring is viewed as a vehicle only for fast-track, young executives, but it can work equally well in the sales force, on the factory floor, or in a functional department, such as accounting or engineering. The willingness of executives at all levels to share their experience and wisdom with younger employees is one characteristic of a PLE.

28. Employees are encouraged and rewarded for outside work in their professions. In many companies with a PLE, employees who write papers for the industry, professional journals, or magazines or who make presentations at conferences are rewarded, both with monetary rewards and with publicity in the company's internal newsletters and magazines. These types of rewards encourage employees to increase their own knowledge, to share that knowledge with others, and to gather new knowledge from others—all signs of a PLE.

29. Employees are constantly on the prowl for best, or better, practices. In companies with a PLE, employees are constantly searching for better ways to do their own jobs and improve group and company business results. Whether gathered from another group within the company or from an outside source, formal and informal benchmarks are constantly in progress. And the people doing the benchmarking are the ones responsible for the work, not a centralized benchmarking group. When employees attend conferences, for example, they may be searching for ways to improve their own or the group's performance. But if they see or hear something that may be of benefit to another group in the company, they will gather the information and send it along to that group, even if they don't know anyone in the group.

30. Employees look forward to meetings. In companies with a PLE, meetings are used to provide information, exchange and discuss ideas, and help the meeting participants learn from each other. Meetings are planned for these purposes and are not held unless there is a clear learning objective that can be communicated before the meeting and measured at the meeting's close.

INDEPENDENT LEARNING IN A COMPANY WITH A PLE

So how do all of these characteristics relate to the movement to ISDL? Only companies that spend the time and effort (and it will require a massive effort in most companies) to build and maintain a PLE will succeed in the movement toward ISDL. When a PLE exists, employees will constantly seek opportunities for learning. And because the PLE exists, they will find those opportunities at every turn.

Without a PLE, employees will not seek learning opportunities, for they will know that there will be little chance to use any new knowledge or skills they acquire. If company managers aren't interested in their ideas, why bother? These employees will turn their learning energies and efforts to outside interests or to finding a new job in a company that has a PLE.

At Rosenbluth International, the company's PLE is one of the major ways that the company attracts employees. The travel industry in general is a low-margin business, and the opportunities for development and growth within the company are a major attractor for new employees and a major contributor to the company's employee-retention rates, which are among the highest in its industry.*

For the movement to ISDL to be successful, it also requires that companies define new roles, responsibilities, and relationships among leaders, managers, and employees. In the next section, we will explore what this means and the roles of all company employees in building and maintaining a PLE.

LEARNING ASSIGNMENT

Review the list of 30 indicators of a positive learning environment (table 2-1). Think of additional indicators of a PLE (not on the table) that you would like to see in your organization. How can you help create a PLE at your company? If you believe that making the indicators happen is not within your power, how can you influence the people in the organization who could make them happen? Take personal responsibility for making them happen or for getting decision makers to consider them.

1. List five indictors of a PLE from table 2-1, which are not present in your organization.

2. Now think of five additional indicators of a PLE (not on the table) that you would like to see in your organization.

3. From these 10 indicators, highlight the three that you consider the most important. How can you as an individual help make those three things happen?

INDICATOR	WHAT CAN I DO TO MAKE IT HAPPEN?
1.	
2.	
3.	

ENDNOTE

* Provided by and printed by permission from Rosenbluth International.

Chapter 3

Making Employees Responsible for Their Own Learning

All learning is self-directed. Whether you are in a classroom, reading, or taking a computer-based training program, you, as the learner, decide what is important to you and, therefore, you choose what you will learn. Making employees responsible for their own learning requires that they be able to

- identify their own learning needs
- find and access the learning resources (both people and materials) they need to undertake that learning
- apply the learning to their work to make a positive difference in their individual, group, and company business results.

Each of these three requirements is very different from the ways in which training has traditionally been done in organizations. To meet each requirement will necessitate major changes, not only in employee skills and behavior, as will be discussed in this chapter, but also in the ways in which managers manage (chapter 4), leaders lead (chapter 5), and trainers train (chapter 6).

IDENTIFYING YOUR OWN LEARNING NEEDS

In a previous job as a training manager, I developed training programs for a large audience of sales, sales-support, and technical-support personnel. I did not conduct a full needs assessment, but I did attempt to identify the topics for training, to be followed by further work to define the content of the training programs. In trying to define these employees' learning needs, I sought information from six main sources.

First, I asked the employees themselves what they believed they needed to learn to do their jobs better. After all, the employees themselves knew better than anyone where they were encountering stumbling blocks in getting their daily work done, what questions customers were asking that they couldn't answer, and what new knowledge and skills would help them better succeed at their jobs. Of course, this method could only uncover their areas of conscious ignorance—what they knew they didn't know. To define other areas of unconscious ignorance—what they didn't know they didn't know— I had to ask others.

Second, I asked managers what new skills and knowledge their employees needed to improve their job performance. This view was frequently similar to that of employees but always included some training needs that the employees themselves didn't see. Sometimes, this resulted from the employees believing that they were doing well on the job while the manager saw that there was room for improvement. Other times, the employees didn't have a view of a reorganization of duties that the manager was planning.

Third, I asked corporate groups, such as product management and marketing, what new products, services, marketing campaigns, and so forth were planned about which the employees and their managers in the field didn't yet have knowledge. This helped me to prepare the employees for future changes.

Fourth, I asked the competitive-analysis group to help define which competitors were giving our company the toughest challenges and which were preparing major challenges to our strategic position, and to help prepare training on how to meet or beat those competitors' challenges.

Fifth, I asked the company's technical-support groups to tell me what questions they were most commonly hearing from the field personnel. These questions often indicated areas in which the field needed further development.

Finally, I asked customers about knowledge and skill areas our company's employees were lacking: what questions our representatives had the hardest time answering, how our representatives compared to personnel from our major competitors, and so forth. This was usually done informally when I attended an industry conference or a trade show and I had an opportunity to talk with the company's customers—admittedly not as frequently as I would have liked. More typically, I relied on customer surveys done by the marketing group for this input.

Of the six information sources I accessed, only the first is readily available to the employee; only the employee's own areas of conscious ignorance immediately jump into the employee's mind as areas for learning. If employees are to take responsibility for their own learning, to determine their own learning needs, and to find the learning resources to meet their learning requirements, they must have access to the information they need to make those determinations. But just as I, as a training manager, had to go to other sources to determine employees' full range of learning needs, so they will have to find ways of tapping these other sources.

In traditional organizations, employees, supported by traditional training and development groups, identify what training they will attend over the next year. Typically, the method of identifying your own learning needs is haphazard at best. The employee sees a course in the company's training catalog, reads about an industry conference that sounds interesting, or receives a piece of direct mail about an external seminar or workshop. When something of interest comes along, the employee goes to his or her manager and asks permission to attend. The manager may respond that the selected program "looks interesting," or may say something like, "Sure, that sounds like a good idea" or "Why not? You haven't been to a program for a while and we have the money in the budget."

Sometimes the idea for a learning opportunity comes from the manager: "I've been reading about this new technique that might be valuable for us. There's a conference going on next month. Why don't you go and see what you can learn about it?"

At other times, training may be a last ditch attempt at saving the employee's job: "Look, this just isn't working out. We've tried to teach you the right way to do things around here, but you just don't seem to get it. I'm going to send you to a company-sponsored training program. If that doesn't work, you'll have to look for another job."

These are all reactions to external stimuli. Less frequently, the manager will sit down with one or more employees and say: "Here's the direction the company is going in. If we want to continue to contribute to (or lead) the company, we've got to be ready for the changes coming down the road. Let's brainstorm about what these changes will mean to the work we are doing, what skills and knowledge we are going to need, and how we can best acquire them. Then we'll come up with a group-learning plan, and from that we'll derive individual-learning plans. We're all in this together, and we need to learn together and implement these new methods and ideas together so that we can all succeed."

Employees must take an active role in picking areas for improvement, identifying new knowledge and skills that will be needed in the future, seeking a range of learning methods that match personal learning styles, developing a plan to obtain the necessary knowledge and skills, and then applying them to the job.

Although the next chapters deal with the roles of managers, leaders, and training groups in helping the employee, the primary responsibility for defining learning needs, doing the learning, and applying that learning will always fall to the employee. One thing is clear: The employee cannot define learning needs in terms of the company's strategic business direction unless the employee understands what that direction is—and most employees don't have a clue on the future directions the company is contemplating or on what those directions mean to their jobs.

LEARNING ABOUT THE COMPANY

If we want employees to take responsibility for their own learning and if we want that learning to contribute to the company's success, we must make certain that all employees have the information they need to plan a rational learning program. This means that employees must understand

- the company's strategic business directions
- the implications of those directions on the work of the employee's business unit, functional group, team, and, ultimately, to the employee's individual work
- how those directions will change the employee's job and the skill and knowledge requirements for that job.

Without this information, how can the employee possibly identify his or her learning needs and develop a rational learning agenda? But in most companies, information about the company's strategic business directions has a very limited distribution—usually just to the top management team. In many cases, when companies try to distribute the information more widely, usually through a top-down approach, lower-level managers hoard the information, never sharing it with their employees. If knowledge is power, many midlevel managers decide to keep the power to themselves and not distribute it to their employees.

Ideally, the company will make a concerted effort to share strate-
gic information with every employee. If the company wants to succeed in making employees responsible for their own learning and if the company wants to ensure that this learning will support the company's strategic business directions, the company has no choice: it must do everything possible to ensure that all employees have the information needed to plan their own learning in support of the company's business goals. Without this information reaching every employee at every level, the movement to ISDL cannot succeed.

If the company doesn't make such an effort or if at some level of the company an information block exists that inhibits the spread of this critical information, what can employees do? How can employees find the information they need to plan their own learning? Even without a formal, company-communication plan for this information, much of it is available to employees if they know where to look and if they take the time to search for it. Some is available inside the company and some outside.

The point is that employees can find the information if they want it. More important, it is vital to the company's success that employees have this information so that they can focus their improvement and learning activities on supporting the company's strategic business directions. The company will make a lot more progress if everyone is headed in the same direction, working toward the same goals. But, if you don't tell employees in which direction you want them to go, you leave to chance which direction they will take, most likely resulting in many people heading in many different directions—not the best way to make progress.

Rather than making employees hunt for the information they need, why not provide it to them? Companies can provide information in many ways, such as the following:

- *Give every employee a copy of the company's annual report.* Follow this with information sessions with top company officers to explain the company's business directions and answer employee questions. With the advent of relatively inexpensive videoconferencing systems and even less expensive computer-conferencing capabilities, even the most geographically-dispersed companies can hold these types of open forums.

- *Open the company's files of press clippings to all employees.* Many companies' corporate-communication groups keep files of press clippings about the company. Typically, these clippings are distributed to top company officers. Why not post them on the company's intranet so that all employees can have access to them?

 - *Set up and use an employee-communication plan.* Such a system can inform employees at all levels about major strategic decisions and plans. Measure (and reward) managers at all levels to ensure that these communications take place without filtering through all levels of the company.

When every employee understands the company's strategic business directions, you have made a good and necessary start to this process. But, taken alone, this is not sufficient to empower employees to undertake their own learning initiatives. The really hard work comes with helping all employees understand their roles in helping to achieve the company's business goals.

UNDERSTANDING YOUR ROLE IN THE COMPANY

In many large companies, employees don't understand the company's major business processes and their roles in those processes. Sometimes, employees don't even know what the company makes or what services the company provides, much less how their individual jobs contribute to the company's workings.

We are All in the Sales Department

Many years ago, I brought an outside speaker into a large training event I was hosting. The audience of 400 people included salespeople, field-support people, and many different corporate groups. The speaker started out with a question: "How many of you are in sales?" All of the sales representatives in the audience (about 40 people) raised their hands.

"Wrong!" shouted the speaker. "You are all in sales." He made a good point. Every company employee, no matter what his or her job title, should be an effective company spokesperson. Whether talking with colleagues at a professional meeting, answering an outside telephone call at work, or chatting with a neighbor, every employee should be able to answer questions about the company and present a positive image of the company and its products or services. But unless we help employees understand the company's business, how can they do this?

It is the job of company leadership and managers at all levels to ensure that their employees understand their role in the company's success. This means explaining the company's business processes and the role of each employee's work in those processes. Further, it is incumbent upon managers to translate company business goals into local or group goals and then into what those goals mean to the jobs of individual employees.

"To help the company achieve its goals, our group is going to have to improve its performance in these ways. That means we will have to find a better way of doing X and Y." This type of explanation goes a long way toward helping individual employees determine their own learning needs. "If I need to find a better way of doing X and Y, I'd better learn about these new procedures and improve my skills in J and K."

The Last Shall Be First

Over the years, I have seen and read about extraordinary performance exhibited by a number of corporate groups whose jobs are typically thought of as dead-end, low-skill, or generally undesirable and whose employees are unrightfully stereotyped as low-intelligence or low-potential.

In one company, the plant-maintenance department won many awards—from the company and from professional and industry groups—for quality improvement and cost reduction. When the maintenance employees were interviewed about their work, they remarked that they held "the most important jobs in the company." Employees liked to come to work because of the excellent condition of the facilities. Industrial accidents were at an all-time low because of the excellent work of the maintenance department. Customers were very impressed with the cleanliness and conditions of the plant.

Although the maintenance departments in most companies go unappreciated, this maintenance group understood how it contributed to company goals and took pride in its work and how that work pleased everyone, employees and customers alike.

In another company, one of my employees worked with the company's credit-and-collections department. Typically, this function rarely gets good press inside or outside the company. Credit personnel are often mistreated by salespeople, who feel like they are holding up their sales, and by customers who don't like being reminded that they have unpaid bills. The turnover in the collections business is very high. But this credit-and-collections department became a top performer in the industry. Why? The department manager helped the employees realize how important the function was to the company's success. "The engineers and the salespeople may get all the glory," she said, "but we're the ones who make certain that the company gets the funds to pay all those people. Without a great performance by this department, our financial results would suffer greatly."

The lesson here is that every group and every employee should be made to feel as if their work counts, that their work makes a real difference to the company's success, and that the excellence of their work can make a real difference to the company's bottom line.

UNDERSTANDING CAREER PATHS WITHIN THE COMPANY

One of the primary learning motivators for employees involves career growth within the company. To be motivated by career growth possibilities, employees need to be aware that

- opportunities may be available within their current job and line of work
- opportunities may become available in other parts of the company for job enlargement or career change
- opportunities may open up within the company as it pursues new lines of business, introduces new technologies, opens up new markets, and so forth.

If employees can understand these opportunities, they must then undertake an assessment of their current skills versus those needed for the desired position, how they can obtain the knowledge and skills needed for those new opportunities, and how they can access those new opportunities as they arise. If these questions are answered and if the employee decides to pursue the new opportunities, motivation will take care of itself.

FINDING AND ACCESSING LEARNING RESOURCES

Assuming that employees are able to identify their learning needs, they must now find and access the learning resources they will need to accomplish their learning goals. Unfortunately, when many companies have moved to ISDL, they greatly reduce or even eliminate their traditional training activities, but fail to give employees help or guidance on how to overcome their longstanding reliance on those training activities. "If I needed to take some training, I just looked in the company's training catalog, picked a course, checked the schedule, and signed up for training. Now there's no catalog, no schedule, nobody to call. What am I supposed to do?"

This isn't employee empowerment, this is employee abandonment. So how can companies help their employees find and access learning resources? Companies have developed many innovative methods, some of which I describe here:

- *Competency Maps.* Ken Pederson at the Dow Chemical Company* says that the company has developed a comprehensive set of competency maps that helps employees plan for their next jobs and helps managers conduct effective interviews based on the competencies needed for each job and the competencies held by the employee. Hubert Saint-Onge, of Canada's Mutual Group, puts it this way: "To support employee learning, you need competency maps for employees. The manager's role is to ensure that employees own their own performance. Managers must own the coaching of their employees. Managers must also move individual employees to self-initiation by spelling out expectations for performance and development; and reviewing on a regular basis achievement of expectations."†

- *Learning Counselors.* Hubert Saint-Onge once set up a network of learning counselors upon whom employees could call for help in identifying learning resources inside and outside the company. At Mercury Marine in Fond du Lac, Wisconsin, training director Joseph Slezac used counselors from the local branch of the University of Wisconsin to provide learning guidance to employees (Tobin 1997).

- *Learning Guides.* Some companies have developed learning guides that employees can use to determine learning methods for a wide variety of learning needs. These learning guides provide pointers to company-sponsored courses and relevant books and articles, as well as suggestions on how to get personal assistance within the company from managers and peers in applying learning to the job.

- *Learning Leaders.* At Rosenbluth International[‡] much learning takes place at local offices led by local leaders in learning (LiL). These individuals track local learning needs and help employees find ways of learning. According to Kathi Keller, manager of the LiL program at Rosenbluth International, LiLs are mainly reservations agents who work as LiLs either part-time or full-time, depending on the size of the office they are supporting. The LiLs do local needs assessments, provide training materials, and often lead short learning programs for groups of employees. Rosenbluth International's corporate-training group trains the LiLs and responds to their requests for materials and methods. The LiLs support each other by exchanging locally developed ideas, methods, and materials.

- *Peer Coaching.* Rosenbluth International also uses peer-to-peer coaching to help employees improve their performance. Suppose, for example, that one employee is not up to Rosenbluth International's standard for customer telephone interaction. That employee may be paired with another employee who excels in this area. At the same time, they will try to choose a coach who can also learn something from the person being coached. For example, the employee may need help with customer interaction but may be a top performer on using the company's computer systems. In selecting a customer-interaction coach for this person, they will try to find someone who could also benefit from learning more about the computer systems, so that the learning goes in both directions.

- *Intranet Access.* At Wang Global, we are creating an intranet site for the corporate-training function that will contain online learning guides, similar to those of PPG Industries described above. These learning guides will also include a wide variety of links to other Websites, links to the course catalog of the American Management Association, online magazines, and reference resources. It will also be linked to our corporate lending-library catalog and the means for ordering materials from that catalog.

At the same time, companies must have learning-supportive policies in place. Many companies pay lip service to employee learning but do little to support employee learning. Although leadership and managerial behaviors will be discussed in subsequent chapters, here are some examples of company policies that can support employee learning:

- Tuition assistance plans should support a wide variety of educational programs and not require employees to lay out large amounts of money up-front for tuition and books and then wait until the course is completed before being reimbursed.

- Professional memberships and subscriptions to professional journals help employees to learn about the latest developments in their professions.

- Support for attending professional and industry conferences and trade shows helps employees to keep abreast of their fields.

- Access to the Internet helps employees conduct their own searches for learning resources.

- Development of a knowledge network (chapter 8) can help employees identify internal and external knowledge resources.

- Corporate membership at a local university library not only supports higher education but can also provide corporate library cards that allow employees to use the university's library.

- Training on mentoring and coaching skills, as well as measurements and rewards for applying those skills, can help leaders and managers guide employee learning and serve as valuable learning resources for employees.

- Measurements and rewards for employee-learning achievements provide incentives (not necessarily monetary) for employee learning.

- Sponsorship of employees to write papers for publication and to make conference presentations encourages employee learning, sharing of knowledge, and recognition of employee achievements.

A DIFFERENT DIMENSION OF LEARNING: LEARNING FROM OTHER EMPLOYEES

Heretofore, companies have focused on traditional forms of learning, such as training, as the means for employees to learn. Employees learn through many avenues that are likely even more significant than formal learning experiences, for example, informal learning, learning from other employees, and sharing knowledge with other employees, in turn.

If learning is defined as the acquisition of information you need to improve your own, your group's, and the company's business performance, then learning takes place in many different ways. For example, have you ever spent hours or days or even weeks solving a problem only to discover later that someone else in the company had already solved it, perhaps with a better solution than you had implemented? If you don't know the person who had previously solved the problem or if you have no way of finding that learning resource, it is as if that person and that solution did not exist. If your company wants to maximize the return on its knowledge assets, it must make it easy for employees to find these learning resources. Building a knowledge network can enable employees to find these resources, whether they consist of a report in the company's knowledge database or the name of a person from whom the employee can learn. But a knowledge network can only work if it exists, if people use it, and if people are willing to share their knowledge and skills with others.

HELPING EMPLOYEES LEARN TO LEARN

The traditional model of corporate-training development has encouraged employees to depend on the training group to identify their learning needs and to meet those needs. With the movement to ISDL, many employees now find themselves unable to even think about how to identify and meet their own learning needs. If we want this movement to work, we need to teach employees how to learn.

Learning, for most employees, takes place every day on the job, but it is an unconscious process. When a colleague demonstrates a feature on a spreadsheet program, when the boss answers a question, when people chat over lunch, learning is happening. But if you ask people how they will learn about a new topic, master a new skill, or learn a new procedure, they may be stumped for an answer.

One way of helping employees learn to learn is to help them identify the many ways in which they are already learning. By raising their learning consciousness, we enable them to consciously repeat the learning processes they have been using for a long time. As will be described in the next chapter, managers can play an important role in this by coaching their employees.

Companies are also well advised to pay attention to issues around employee literacy when moving toward ISDL. Functional literacy still remains a large challenge for businesses around the world. Although someone may be doing a job well and may have learned skills well from an instructor in a classroom, it doesn't mean that that employee will automatically have the reading skills needed to use self-paced, print-based, or computer-based learning materials.

Another invaluable set of skills for employees is critical-thinking skills. Basically, critical thinking helps people identify the assumptions under which they have been working and to question those assumptions. For example, someone may ask: "Why do we continue to do this procedure in this way?" A typical answer might be: "Because we have always done it this way, and it works." The reliance on the old saw, "If it ain't broke, don't fix it," typifies this attitude and has probably blocked more individual and corporate progress than can be measured.

Whether you call it paradigm shifting, business-process reengineering, or breaking out of the box, critical thinking enables employees to examine old assumptions and find new and better ways of meeting their individual, group, and corporate goals—and it can all be classified as learning.

If we want employees to direct their own learning, we have to start by teaching them some basic skills on how to identify their learning needs, how to find the resources to meet those needs, and how to learn what needs to be learned. But if we want to ensure that all of this learning makes a positive difference in individual and organizational performance, we must go beyond these basic requirements to ensure that what is learned gets applied and applied correctly to the employees' work.

APPLYING LEARNING TO THE EMPLOYEE'S WORK

When describing the four-stage learning model (figure 1-1), I stated that information becomes knowledge by applying it to your work. Unless the employee soon applies new information or skills, the employee will most likely forget what has been learned, resulting in little if any return on the learning investment, either for the individual or for the company.

Even with formal, company-directed training programs, this is the step where training most often fails: Most of what is taught in the classroom is never applied to the job, thereby voiding the company's investment in the training program. We can hope that if an employee undertakes independent learning on a subject it will increase the likelihood of applying that learning to the job, but this is not necessarily true. In today's interconnected business world, few employees really have the power to radically change the ways in which they work without approval from a manager or from other members of their teams and workgroups. If it is difficult for the company to mandate changes, it will be even more difficult for an individual to do so.

This can be the greatest stumbling block for a movement to ISDL: If employees undertake such learning, but are barred from applying that learning to their jobs, they may give up on doing any learning. Or if they finish their learning program and then face difficulty with its implementation on the job and find no help and no support from managers or peers, they may simply revert back to the old ways of doing things. How can we increase the likelihood that the employee's learning will get applied to the job? This can happen in several ways:

- If management agrees to the changes in job design and work methods *before* the employee undertakes the learning, there is a much greater likelihood that the learning will improve performance.

- The employee may negotiate with the learning resource, such as an instructor, the author of a book, or the provider of a media-based training program, to provide some ongoing coaching after the completion of the program. In this way, when the inevitable questions arise, the employee has a source for answers.

The employee can recruit others in the workgroup or team (including the manager) to undertake the learning together. In this way, because several people will be learning the same material and then trying to apply it, they can coach and reinforce each other. Note that while this strategy can be very effective, it may negate the term "independent learning."

As with any learning activity, the possibility always exists that the employee will find after completing the learning that the new method is not better than the current method and may choose not to implement it. Just because something is new doesn't automatically mean that it is better.

THE ROLE OF COMPANY LEADERS AND MANAGERS

As has already been pointed out, employees alone cannot make ISDL a winning strategy for the company. The company's leaders and managers must create a PLE and must actively assist employees in identifying and accessing the learning resources they require and, later, in applying their learning to their jobs. In the next chapter, I will describe the role of managers in this process.

LEARNING ASSIGNMENT

As an individual learner, think about the last company-sponsored training program or course that you attended. Ask yourself these questions:

- If the company had not mandated your attendance, would you have attended voluntarily?

- Was this program or course your highest-priority learning need? If not, why did you attend this program and not undertake a learning activity tied to that highest-priority need?

- Did you apply the learning from that course to make a positive difference in your own or your group's performance? If not, what prevented you from applying the learning?

- If the company had not provided this course, how would you have found the learning resources needed to learn the content?

- What if your company threw out its training catalog? How would you identify learning opportunities?

Now think from the company's perspective and answer these questions:

- How can the company help individual employees identify their own learning needs?

- How can the company help individual employees find and access the learning resources they need?

- How can the company help employees apply their learning to their jobs?

ENDNOTES

* Provided by and printed by permission from Ken Pederson, Dow Chemical Company.

† Provided by and printed by permission from Hubert Saint-Onge, Canada's Mutual Group.

‡ Provided by and printed by permission from Rosenbluth International.

Chapter 4

The Manager's Role in Independent Learning

No single group of individuals within a company exerts greater control over the success or failure of the movement to ISDL than managers. They can make or break the program. When managers take an active role in defining and meeting the learning needs of their employees, they are mastering the most powerful and effective motivator available to any manager—the employee's personal growth.

Role of the Managers in Training at Wang Global

To train 2,000 MCSEs and MCSDs in only three years, Wang Global decided to use computer-based training as the medium; the recruitment of students for the programs was well underway when I arrived. Managers had been asked to nominate employees for these programs and had responded with hundreds of nominations. Shortly after my arrival, acceptance letters were sent to all nominees. But something was going wrong—many of those accepted into the program weren't

(continued on next page)

signing up. When we followed up with the employees who hadn't responded, we found that some of them didn't know anything about the program, didn't know that they were nominated, didn't know what the company expected from them, and some of them weren't interested in the program.

About 60 days into my new job, we had to present the program and its progress to the company's senior operations committee. When we presented the numbers, a member of the committee asked how we were accepting people into the program. We said that all people nominated into the program had been accepted into it. "How are you notifying them?" he asked. We responded, "We send them individual acceptance letters to either their home or work addresses."

"That's not the way to do it," he told us. "You need to send the letter to the employee's manager. Then have the manager call the employee in and tell him or her, 'We've got this great opportunity for you. This is going to be one of the highest growth areas for the company and we want you to be a part of it. We're ready to invest in you, and we'd like you to invest some of your time in this training to help both your own career and the company grow.'"

This was my first contact with the company's senior operations committee, and I was impressed. Directly involving the managers in signing up students for the program made a tremendous difference in our enrollment rates.

THE MANAGER'S ROLE

If the movement to ISDL is to succeed, managers at all levels need to get deeply involved with their employees' learning efforts. They can do this by

- helping employees understand their roles in meeting group and company business goals
- guiding employees as they explore career paths and then defining learning requirements that will help them achieve both their own career objectives and the company's business goals

- working with employees as they identify and access the learning resources they need to meet their learning, career, and business goals
- ensuring that their employees' learning is applied to their work
- coaching employees
- teaching employees.

For many managers, these are new roles. Let's look at each role and what it means to the job of managers.

I. HELPING EMPLOYEES UNDERSTAND THEIR ROLES IN THE COMPANY

If we want employees to take responsibility for their own learning and ensure that that learning focuses on the needs of the company and the employees' own career needs, we need to help them understand the company's strategic business directions and their roles in helping the company to achieve those business goals. We also need to help them understand how helping the company achieve its business goals will help them achieve their personal goals. The movement to ISDL will be successful only when employees believe that they can reach their personal goals by helping the company achieve its goals. Managers are in a uniquely effective position to make this linkage between the employee's and company's goals in the employee's mind.

Keeping Ahead of the Demand at Wang Global

In the best of all possible worlds, a company's training programs are synchronized with the demand for trained employees; employees are trained just as the need for their new knowledge and skills emerges. But, we rarely live in the best of all possible worlds, and Wang Global needed to respond to the projected, rather than the actual, needs of the Microsoft practices. This meant that we had to make assumptions about the specific skills that would be needed, the numbers of people who would be needed, where they would be needed, and so forth.

(continued on next page)

Keeping Ahead of the Demand at Wang Global
(continued)

Given the reality of the situation, we faced the problems we knew we would face, and we made the programs as dynamic as possible so that we could respond quickly to the ever changing business situation. As soon as there was a critical mass of Microsoft business practices in place, I started a dialogue with the practice managers and made many midcourse corrections so that we could start supporting those businesses directly.

HELPING EMPLOYEES DEVELOP THEIR LEARNING PLANS

It is not enough for managers to tell employees that they need to learn and that the learning will help them with their personal career growth and help the company meet its business goals. Managers must move to the next step by helping employees identify specific learning requirements, as well as the learning resources that will lead to the fulfillment of those requirements.

It's not enough to say, "The company is heading north, so you should plan to move north along with us." Employees, especially those who had relied on the corporate-training group to specify what training was required and when and where the training would occur, need more guidance from their managers. They need to know: "If we're heading north, should I take the bus or a plane? Which route will get me there the fastest? Am I going to be doing the same thing up north, or do I need to learn to adapt to a new climate? I have a real fear of flying—how else can I make the trip?"

Once the company's business goals have been translated down to the business unit and group level, the manager must sit with the employee to discuss and negotiate changes needed in the employee's work to help achieve the group and corporate goals and what the employee needs to learn to effect those changes. Figure 4-1 depicts a learning contract that can provide a framework for these discussions (Tobin 1997). At the end of this chapter, you will be asked to complete

Employment for Life or Employability for Life?

With the rapidly changing business conditions across the globe over the past several decades, with the massive layoffs, plant closings, mergers and acquisitions, few, if any, companies can offer their employees employment for life. Employment for life was rarely stated in any company's employee handbook or philosophy statement, but it was a *de facto* standard for many companies. When I started working for Digital Equipment Corporation in 1981, it was understood that unless I failed badly at my job, I would never have to look outside the company for other employment. Employees at many companies understood that they had a similar, albeit tacit, agreement with their employers.

Companies today choose their words carefully when telling their employees about continued employment at the company. When pushing a training initiative, it is common for attorneys to tell companies what they may and what they may not say to employees. Companies may say, "This new training initiative can help your career," or "This new initiative can help the company." They may not say, "This new training initiative can help your career with the company." The latter statement represents a commitment to the employee that most employers today are not willing to make, for it can lead to lawsuits if the company ever has to lay off the employee.

So, if the company cannot promise lifetime employment, what incentive can it offer to the employee to invest in training? The correct term today is "employability for life," meaning that acquiring new knowledge and skills will help the employee remain employable whether that employment is with the current employer or elsewhere.

I sometimes find myself on the horns of a dilemma. As a training professional, I find it challenging to motivate employees to learn using the new language. Nevertheless, as a corporate manager, I understand the need to avoid contractual commitments that can lead to litigation. It's a matter of balance.

---

a learning contract for yourself or for a "typical" manager in your company to help you understand better what goes into a learning contract and, at the same time, reflect on how managers need to learn to adapt to their changing roles as described in this chapter.

Figure 4-1. The learning contract.

PART I: DEFINE LEARNING NEEDS

1. Understand the company's business goals
2. Translate company goals into group and individual goals
3. Determine what you need to change to meet those goals
4. Determine what you need to learn to make those changes

PART II: DEVELOP A LEARNING PLAN

5. Identify learning resources to be used
6. Identify learning methods to be used
7. Develop a schedule for learning activities
8. Determine methods of measuring learning achievement

PART III: APPLY LEARNING TO WORK AND MEASURE RESULTS

9. Determine how learning will be applied to the job
10. Measure effects of learning on accomplishment of individual, group, and company goals

Of course, for managers to be able to lead their employees through this process means that they must have the information they need to guide their employees and the skills to hold such discussions. This is rarely the case. The topic of the next chapter is the role of company leadership in making the needed information available to employees, and later in this chapter, I will discuss what learning managers need to undertake themselves so that they can include these new skills in their management toolbox.

HELPING EMPLOYEES IDENTIFY AND ACCESS LEARNING RESOURCES

The next part of the learning contract includes two key items:

- how the employee should undertake that learning: availability of learning resources, access to those resources, schedule for the learning activities, and so forth
- how learning achievement will be measured.

Helping employees identify their learning needs is a start but is not sufficient to ensure the successful empowerment of employees to undertake ISDL. Managers must move on to help employees identify available learning resources and to help them to access those resources.

The traditional methods of corporate training and development made employees dependent on the corporate-training organization to define what they would learn, how they would learn it, and when they would learn it. In this new era, employees find, schedule, and access a wide variety of learning resources on their own. Although it is possible that employees could accomplish this strictly on their own, it behooves the company to provide some assistance and, since the training organization probably doesn't have the resources needed to counsel employees individually, it falls to the manager to provide this service. Realistically, the manager is the person in the best position to help the employee with this task, for it is the manager who best knows the employee, the employee's current work performance, and what will be required of the employee in the future—things that even the largest, best-funded training organization will never be able to do as well as the manager can.

Again, managers may well find themselves in the position of not having the information or skills needed to fulfill these responsibilities. As will be discussed later in this chapter, the necessary information must be made available to managers; managers need training to handle these new responsibilities.

ENSURING THAT EMPLOYEE LEARNING IS APPLIED TO THE JOB

The final section of the learning contract contains two items that are rarely found today in any employee development plan:

- how the learning will be applied to the employee's work
- what changes in individual, group, and corporate results are expected from the above activities.

These two items are the keys to success. Too often, the learning that employees undertake never gets applied to their work. This means that the investment in learning is totally wasted. Think about the last training program you attended. How much of its content did you immediately apply to your work when you returned to your office? Now, some months later, how much of it are you still using? And how has your learning affected your job performance and your group's and the company's business results? In most cases, your answers to these questions will be "little or none." If there is little or no transfer of training back to the job, and if there are no measurable results of the training, why bother?

Only the employees and their managers can ensure that employee learning is relevant to the job, that newly acquired skills and knowledge are applied to the employee's work, and that the learning results in improvements in individual, group, and company performance. The training group can't do it. Top company officers can't do it. The employee, working in isolation, will find it very difficult to do. Only the manager, working with the employee, can make it all work.

OTHER NEW ROLES FOR MANAGERS

As if the above new responsibilities for managers with regard to employee learning weren't enough, I will add two more new roles and skill sets to the manager's job description: coaching employees and teaching employees.

The Manager as Coach

A coach is someone who has frequent opportunities to observe an employee's work and offer tips on how to improve job performance. The coach's role may include teaching and certainly includes reinforcement of proper performance. The coach's job is to comment on areas of poor or less-than-perfect performance and to make suggestions on how to improve, but the coach can also make employees aware of areas of unconscious competence—areas where employees perform well but don't realize that they have certain skills. When employees become aware of these strengths, they can then build on those strengths.

It is not necessary for the coach to be an expert in every area of the employee's job nor is it necessary for the coach to be the employee's only, or even primary, source of learning. But when a coach sees an area of the employee's performance that needs improvement, the coach should be able to help the employee identify and access the right learning resources. The coach can provide such resources or direct the employee to sources within the group or elsewhere inside or outside the company. This extends the role of manager beyond being a job coach to also being a learning coach. The manager, as learning coach, may say such things as

- "Here's an article I recently came across that has some ideas you might be able to use. Why don't you read the article and think about it? Then we can sit down and talk about the ideas, see which of them might make sense for our group, and develop a plan for trying them out."

- "Mary Smith over in purchasing used to work for me and had a way of doing this procedure that I never understood, but it gave some really great results. Why don't you give Mary a call and set up a meeting? Tell her I told you to call. Then come on back and we'll talk about it."

- "At a conference I attended last week, Joe Brown of Brown Enterprises talked about some of the great things they are doing there in improving customer retention. Although their industry is very different from ours, I think some of the ideas might work here. I'd like to arrange a site visit for you to go over there and see what you can learn that can help us with our work here."

The numbers of ways in which a manager can coach an employee are endless. Coaching takes time and work on the part of the manager, and coaching generally falls outside the traditional duties of a manager. To be effective in this new coaching role, the manager must

- develop his or her own network of learning resources
- keep up with developments within and without the group and the company
- have the humility to say, "I don't have the answer, but maybe we can find it together"
- learn to diagnose employee performance difficulties
- learn how to coach employees in a supportive, nonthreatening manner

- allow employees to learn on the job and fail on the job—a necessary part of learning.

It's not always possible for a manager to know everything necessary to coach an employee effectively. In these cases, it is important for the manager to know where to find coaching assistance for the employee. Sometimes this is another manager or another employee in the group. At other times, it is someone outside the group or even outside the company. Directing a manager to such sources may take the form of

- "Sally has done a lot of work in this area. Why don't you spend some time with her and see if she can give you some tips?"
- "There's a trade show in town next month, and they have a long list of sessions and exhibitors of interesting products that could help you and the group as a whole. Why don't you plan to spend a day there and see what you can learn?"
- "I recently received an email from our professional association about its new Website. They've got a lot of information and education resources. Why don't you check out the Website? If you can't find what you need there, send an email to the association's training manager and see what he can suggest."
- "There was a piece in the last company newsletter about a guy in our German subsidiary who has a unique approach to this problem that works for them. Send him an email and see what you can find out."

In a later section of this chapter, I will discuss the manager's own learning requirements. Chapter 8 addresses how a knowledge network can help managers in this role.

Teaching Employees

Most managers do some teaching. For newly hired employees, managers spend a lot of time teaching. Some first-line supervisors spend as much as half their time teaching job skills to new hires. An expectation exists, however, that once an employee has worked at a job for some period of time, he or she should have mastered the job and no longer require as much time or teaching from the manager.

If ISDL is to succeed, managers will have to assume more responsibilities for directing the learning of their employees, if not teaching them directly. Even when an employee undertakes an ISDL course of study, it is incumbent upon the manager to know enough about the subject to ensure that the employee's learning is relevant to the job, that the learning is applied correctly to the job, that questions that arise as learning is applied are answered (by the manager or by someone else), and that the learning and its application actually add value to the work of the employee and the group. The manager should also be an exemplar of the new approaches: "Do as I do."

These are all characteristics of a good teacher. Teaching does not always imply a classroom or formal instruction. Years ago, when I taught mathematics at a junior high school, the most effective teaching interactions I had were not when I taught a lesson to the whole class, but when I spent time reviewing the work of individual students, helping them to correct misperceptions as they did their work, emphasizing the finer points as they applied the principles to different types of problems, or suggesting a different approach when they didn't understand the first explanation. These are all roles that the manager should play.

As I make presentations on these new roles for managers, I often hear complaints from my audience. Clearly, the manager cannot know everything that every employee needs to learn nor are there enough hours in the day to keep track of every employee's work and learning plans. Nevertheless, managers can use other strategies to encourage and reinforce employee learning.

OTHER MANAGEMENT STRATEGIES

One of the most effective strategies in helping to encourage employee learning is for managers to admit that they don't know everything and that they have much to learn. Sharing in employees' learning activities can be a great motivator. To initiate joint learning, the manager can say:

- "I don't know the answer to that question. Can you do some research to find the answer? Here are some places to start searching. When you find the answer, please let me know so that I can learn along with you."

- "Let's see if we can learn about this together. Then we can teach the rest of the group. There's a class next month at the local college. Why don't we both sign up for it?"

- "I'm not sure what the answer is, but let me see what I can find out. Then I'll let you know."

A number of other effective strategies are available to the manager who is helping employees move toward ISDL. For example, when the group has a learning need, assign more than one person to learn about the subject by whatever learning method is chosen. If two employees take the same course, they can coach each other as they try to apply their learning to their work. Conversely, the manager can assign different learning tasks to different employees with the explicit expectation that they will teach their newly learned skills to the others in the group, including the manager.

When employees go to a conference or a trade show, the manager should make certain that they share the learning with others upon their return. This can be done by sharing papers and presentations from the speakers, by circulating literature and samples collected, or by making a presentation to the group. Many conferences now sell tapes of the presentations; the employee should have a budget for purchasing tapes of some of the better presentations and circulating them to the group. These learning strategies can be made even more effective if group members review the agenda before the conference and give the person who will attend a list of questions to be answered or presentations they would like to hear. Better yet, two or three people can attend the conference with a list of all sessions you would like to have them attend. Then they can report to the group on the sessions so that all benefit.

PREPARING MANAGERS FOR NEW ROLES

Many times, companies have said to managers, "We're going to make some radical changes in the ways in which we work. These changes will have a major effect on your employees. To ease their way along this new path, we need you to coach them, to teach them, to help them succeed." What most companies have failed to understand is that they are requiring the managers themselves to change their own long-standing work methods; coaching and teaching employees are new skills for most managers. Who is going to help the managers? Managers also need help in order to succeed. And yet few companies offer the managers any assistance at all in preparing for these new roles.

In a company that has a PLE, every employee is a learner—no matter if that employee is called an accountant, a shipping-room clerk, a manager, or a vice president. Too often, companies ignore the learning needs of managers and executives. The learning contract shown in figure 4-1 applies equally to the lowest-level employee and to the company president.

To make the movement to ISDL succeed, every employee at every level must have a learning contract. Employees won't succeed if they don't receive coaching from their managers, and managers won't succeed unless they receive coaching from their managers.

Teaching Coaching Skills at Wang Global

Development of coaching skills is one of those subjects that would seem to demand live, instructor-led instruction. With the rush to save money by replacing classroom training with media-based instruction, many companies have come out with workbooks, CD-ROMs, and intranet-based courses on the subject. Can they do the job or is instructor interaction really required?

As I write, we are trying an experiment at Wang Global. Building coaching skills is one of the highest priorities of the training group that I manage, yet we have very little funding available for classroom instruction. I have reviewed six or so self-paced, coaching-skills programs that are available on various media. I personally consider most of them a waste of time and money, but I have found a few that did quite a good job in presenting the subject matter.

The problem remains that these media-based programs, no matter how good, cannot replace a live instructor. With a live instructor, students can bring in their war stories, can talk about good and bad experiences, and can ask for advice on situations they are facing on the job. None of these opportunities can be made available on a CD-ROM.

(continued on next page)

Our future plans at Wang Global include three main components. We will make a media-based, coaching-skills program available on CD-ROM and on our training Website on the company's intranet. We will hold scheduled chat sessions during which employees who have gone through the instruction can bring their questions, swap their experiences, and discuss their dilemmas. Either a senior HR manager, who has a background in coaching skills, or I will host these sessions. We will also do a Train-the-Trainer session for HR representatives and give them a set of exercises and role-playing exercises that they can use for short, field-based training sessions for people who have completed the media-based program.

Will this approach be as effective as bringing managers into a central training facility for a weeklong coaching skills training program? Probably not. Will this approach help raise the level of coaching skills among the company's managers? Most likely yes, if it is done well and if managers participate in all three components of the program. The experiment at Wang Global hasn't yet begun, but we await the results eagerly.

Managers are employees too, and their learning needs require equal attention if the movement to ISDL is to have a chance of succeeding.

LEARNING ASSIGNMENT

Are managers in your company ready for the roles described in this chapter? Complete a learning contract (figure 4-1) for yourself, or for a typical manager in your company, to meet a corporate business goal of implementing ISDL.

Once you have completed the learning contract, discuss with other managers in your company how you can best prepare managers for the new roles described in this chapter. How can ISDL be used to meet these managers' learning needs?

The Manager's Learning Contract

PART I: DEFINE LEARNING NEEDS

1. The company's stated goal is to develop the use of ISDL by employees at all levels to reduce the cost of training and to help the company reach its stated business goals.
2. Write one or more goals for yourself (or for a typical company manager) that reflect what you need to do to support this corporate goal.
3. What specific behavior do you need to adopt (or change) to meet these personal goals?
4. What new knowledge or skills do you need to acquire to enable you to meet these personal goals?

PART II: DEVELOP A LEARNING PLAN

5. What learning resources are available to you or can you find to help you acquire the knowledge and skills specified above?
6. What learning methods will you use?
7. Develop a schedule for the specified learning activities: "I will complete which activity by which date?"
8. How will I measure my learning?

PART III: APPLY LEARNING TO WORK AND MEASURE RESULTS

9. How will you apply the learning to your job?
10. How will you know whether you have met your personal learning goals and whether these have helped the company achieve its stated goal of reducing training costs and enabling employees to help the company achieve its business goals?

Chapter 5

Leadership's Role in Independent Learning

The move to ISDL, as is the case with any major change effort, will succeed or fail based on the quality of leadership for the effort. Although leadership, by definition, emanates from any and all levels of the organization, I will focus here on the role of top company leadership, the roles of lower-level management having been discussed in the chapter 4.

The company's top-management team often initiates the movement to ISDL. In many companies, top management, having become dissatisfied by the results of traditional training efforts, seeing ever-increasing budgets but few results, reduces the company's training budget or, in some extreme cases, shuts down the training organization and tells employees that they are now responsible for their own learning. This may reduce expenditures dramatically, but, in and of itself, does little to ensure that ISDL will succeed.

How can the organization's top leaders ensure that the movement to ISDL will help achieve company goals? How can they build a PLE? How can they make continuous learning a top priority for every employee in the organization? Although many methods will be discussed in this chapter, they all fall under four primary categories:

- ensuring that every employee knows how his or her job relates to company goals
- modeling of learning activities by top managers
- encouraging employee learning at all levels
- building an organization-wide infrastructure to support learning.

COMMUNICATING COMPANY GOALS

If all employees are to align their learning activities with the company's goals, employees must understand those goals and how their work affects those goals. Without this basic understanding, ISDL (and more traditional forms of training) cannot help the company. The most important job for company leadership is to help every employee achieve this understanding.

In many companies, leaders communicate with the top of the management structure and assume (or mandate) that managers apprise their employees of the company's goals. In too many companies, the information never wends its way through the management structure. To achieve this goal, leaders must do two things:

- They must take every opportunity to inform employees about the company's goals and how their individual and group work relates to those goals.
- They must measure and reward managers based on how well they carry out their communications objectives.

At the same time, they must constantly monitor the situation to ensure that the communications takes place. When walking through the factory floor, when visiting a sales office, when speaking at a functional meeting, leaders must take every opportunity to reinforce their message about company goals and test employee understanding of those goals. If employees don't understand the company's goals and how their work relates to those goals, the alignment of their learning activities to support those goals will be serendipitous at best or, worse, won't happen at all.

MODELING OF LEARNING ACTIVITIES BY TOP MANAGERS

It is not enough for the organizations leadership to write a memorandum or give a speech to employees about how important and valuable their learning activities are to the organization. Leaders must walk the talk; they must demonstrate that they themselves are in a continuous learning mode.

Do as I Say, Not as I Do

Several years ago, I consulted to a high-technology manufacturers' educational-services group. The company had a beautiful training facility located across a large parking lot from corporate headquarters—a five-minute walk. One of the group's most important activities was a three-day seminar for customers' chief technology officers (CTOs). Part education and part marketing, the seminars were an important activity for the educational-services group and for the company as a whole.

When these seminars were held, the educational-services group always invited the company's CEO or another of its top officers to spend a couple of hours with the group, usually during lunch on the last day. Two important purposes were served by this interaction. First, it gave the seminar participants some high-level attention. After all, these were the people who made the decisions as to whether to buy the company's products and services or whether to do business with the company's competitors. Second, the interaction gave the company's leaders exposure to the company's customers and their concerns, so that they could learn from the customers.

According to the group leader, the top executives didn't show up about half the time, often without informing anyone that they weren't going to be there. What message did this send to the customers in the seminar? What message did it send to company employees about the importance of learning from the customers? Given this type of behavior on the part of the company's top executives, it was not surprising that learning activities were not valued generally by the company, nor was it any great revelation that the company's fortunes were on the decline.

Effective leaders participate in many learning activities themselves. They visit and talk with customers. They attend trade shows and industry conferences, not just to spread the word about their own company, but to learn about what the competition is doing. They belong to industry associations to share ideas with their peers. They discuss, plan, and implement new ideas with their peers and their staffs within the company. They make all of these activities visible to people throughout the company.

Just as the executives of the previously described high-technology company clearly demonstrated that they didn't value talking with customers, effective learning leaders make their customer interactions visible to others in the company. They make it clear that learning from customers is so valued that they themselves spend time doing it. They take what they learn and bring it back to discuss with others: "Here's what I heard from the customer. Are we addressing the problems the customer raised? Does the customer's idea for a new product make sense? Is there a market for that new product beyond that single customer? Let's put a team together to investigate and report on the idea so that we can make a decision."

It takes courage and humility for an organization's top leaders to admit that they have their own learning needs. Too often, a company's top leaders believe that they must have all the answers and that to admit a learning need would be to admit weakness. What those leaders must recognize is that setting an example as a learner will encourage others to learn and will lead to greater rather than less respect. Polly Labarre (1999) tells the story of Pillsbury's CEO: "The current CEO, Paul Walsh, came to the job from finance. He had none of the marketing experience that's so critical to running a consumer-products company. The first thing he did was to admit to that knowledge gap; he then created a plan to learn everything he could about marketing. Because he was so open, people enthusiastically helped him."

Reading books and articles are part of leadership's own learning. When a leader reads a book or article that sparks some new idea, he or she can share the reading material with others, suggesting that they read the material and then gather together to discuss it: "Do the ideas apply to the company's situation? What can we learn from other companies' experiences? Is there something we can do with one or more of the ideas in the book or article to help improve our own business results?" Buying copies of a book or magazine and distributing them to other staff members is a good start, but it requires follow-up meetings to ensure that the ideas receive proper evaluation. Scheduling a follow-up meeting also helps to ensure that people will actually read the material.

Leaders who use this strategy must be careful not to overdo it. I have seen more than one company in which the CEO or chairman is an avid reader and literally floods the executive suite with books and articles. When this happens, most of the reading material goes unread: "Why bother? We'll just get another book next week. This book is the 'flavor of the week,' to be replaced every week with another flavor. Nobody takes it seriously."

A group of business-book publishers has even gone so far as to start an initiative called Business Literacy 2000 to encourage reading in the workplace. As described by Tom Brown (1999) on the "MG—The New Ideas Website":

> The idea of "Business Literacy 2000" is to bring the reading group concept that has sprung up in living rooms, libraries, and bookstores across the country into the business arena. We have designed this program to encourage groups of business people working inside or outside of organizations to come together to read and discuss the latest business books, to share ideas, to stimulate their own thinking. Our dream is to build a national community of business readers, to take business book publishing to an extraordinary new level of idea-sharing, and, ultimately, to facilitate the use of the ideas in these books to make organizations better places to work.*

When I raised this idea with one CEO, she objected, saying, "I don't have time to do all this, no matter how desirable it may seem. I'm too busy running the business on a day-to-day basis." I responded, "If you are going to lead the company, what more important role can you play than the introduction of new ideas and the stimulation of people throughout the company to discuss your, their own, and others' ideas for improving the company's business results?" She said that she couldn't argue with that and that she would have to reexamine her priorities.

You don't have to be the CEO to use these ideas. Several times a month, I run across a new book, read a review, or peruse an article that I think might be of interest to others in the company. Using email or interoffice mail, I often send notes to anyone—from the CEO on down—who I think may find it to be of some value. Many times I don't get an acknowledgement, but other times I get a note back thanking me and saying that the recipient found the article or book of great value.

In chapter 2, I posed the question: "How would you feel if your CEO walked into your office and found you reading a book?" Let me turn the question around for CEOs and other top company leaders: "How would you react if you walked into an employee's office and found him or her reading a book?" It's not a trick question, but a real measure of how much you value learning in your company. Would your reaction be: "Why aren't you working? Why are you wasting your time reading"? If so, you send a strong message that you don't value learning. On the other hand, would your reaction be: "What's that you're reading? I don't think I've seen that book. Is it any good? Any ideas that can help us"? If these are your questions, you are spreading the word that learning is valued, that new ideas are welcome, and that you appreciate employees who are trying to improve themselves and add value to the company.

ENCOURAGING EMPLOYEE LEARNING

When leaders encourage employee learning, they find that they have mastered the most powerful motivational tool available in today's workplace—the employee's personal growth. When we surveyed a sample of the students within Wang Global Virtual University studying for Microsoft certifications, we found that those who were making the fastest progress through their studies and examinations stated that their managers' continual reinforcement of the importance of achieving certification was a great motivator.

In the classic book, *In Search of Excellence,* Thomas Peters and Robert Waterman (1988) discuss the practice of "management by wandering around" or MBWA. They argue that effective managers get out into the field, down on the shop floor, and around to various company facilities. They make themselves visible by asking and answering questions and seeing for themselves what is happening throughout the company.

Learning leaders can use MBWA to spread the message that learning is valued. They ask questions so that they can learn from their employees. They answer questions, even holding impromptu forums to encourage questions. They raise new ideas for discussion. They ask employees what they think can be improved and how. They spend time sharing their own experiences, discussing what they have been hearing from customers, announcing new initiatives, and so forth. Not only will this demonstrate that the leaders are walking the talk, but it will encourage employees at all levels to share their ideas and to spend time learning, if only to be able to answer questions the next time the boss comes around or to have a good question ready for the boss's next visit.

It was Just an Idea!

The CEOs and other top company leaders must be careful in practicing MBWA that what they say to employees to encourage their thinking isn't automatically understood to be an order. The CEO of one high-technology company often walked through an engineering-group site on Saturdays, stopping to chat with those people who were working that day. More than once, he stopped to chat with a young engineer, asking what the person was working on. After the engineer described what she was working on, the CEO might offer a suggestion or say, "Have you thought about doing it this way?"

After the CEO left, the young engineer found herself in a quandary: "I thought I had a good solution, and my manager agreed. But if the CEO says to do it this other way, maybe I'd better start from scratch." Of course, this isn't what the CEO intended. He was merely being friendly and trying to encourage the young employee. His positional power and his legend in the company made his words sound like an order.

It is important for leaders to make it clear when they introduce a new idea that it is just that—an idea—and maybe it is a poor idea at that. Unless the leader means to issue an order, which should be made clear from the start, ideas for evaluation should be evaluated, with some being accepted and others being rejected or changed through the dialogue process.

If you want to encourage learning, become a teacher. When a company leader teaches in a company-training program, it is immediately obvious to everyone involved that what is being taught it important. The waterfall approach to training, in which CEOs teach their staff, the staff then teach their staff, and so forth, eventually reaching lower and lower levels of the organization, can be very effective. But this method cannot typically be viewed as ISDL.

When someone comes to you with a problem or for a decision, you can use the moment as a teaching opportunity. Don't just solve the problem or make the decision, share your thought process with them: "The way I see this problem is . . ." or "The reason I am making this decision is because . . ." It is one thing to make a decision; it is another to help the person who came to you to learn how to analyze problems and, in the future, make wise decisions him- or herself.

Becoming a mentor can be part of a formal corporate succession-planning process or can be an effective means of helping to identify and prepare future company leaders. In chapter 4, I discussed the manager's role of coach. Although leaders can also take on a coaching role, the role of mentor is somewhat different.

Whereas coaching involves observing the employee's work and offering guidance and instruction on how to improve the employee's performance, mentoring helps the employee understand the organization's culture, how the business really works, and opens the employee's view of career paths within the company. And although a coach can be a direct manager, a peer, a subordinate, or someone from another part of or outside of the organization, a mentor is typically at least two levels higher in the organization than the mentee. How can mentors help mentees?

A very, very narrow definition of "mentor"

- By educating mentees about the culture and norms of the organization, mentors help the mentees better understand the context of their work and careers. For example, mentors may discuss their own career paths with mentees over lunch once a month or so. Mentors may also wish to address the careers of other top company leaders and advise mentees about facing and resolving political problems.
- By identifying growth opportunities that will give mentees exposure to other parts of the company, mentors help mentees

learn more about themselves and about others in the company. Mentors can suggest that mentees take leading roles for the United Way campaign or fill in for other executives who will be away on leave for a time.

• By helping mentees explore career options within their companies, mentors can help guide the mentees' personal and professional growth. For example, a mentor can suggest that an accountant working in the company's sales group could learn more about the company's overall business by making a lateral move into the accounting department of the company's manufacturing operation.

Holding a town meeting for employees, reflecting on the directions the company is taking, asking for feedback from employees, and answering employee questions can be a very effective method of both teaching and demonstrating the value that the company places on learning from employees. With the decreasing price and increasing availability of teleconferencing, videoconferencing, and computer conferencing, such town meetings are becoming more and more common. But, if you want to make them really effective as teaching and learning tools, you need to ensure that the atmosphere is open to any and all questions. You cannot screen questions, and you cannot refuse to answer questions, even if they touch on sensitive areas.

Listen and Learn

In the 1980s, when I ran the Network University program for Digital Equipment Corporation, the vice president of networks and communications would hold frequent, open forums for hundreds of participants from around the world. He would open with an update on the latest happenings in the networks and communications world at Digital, and then he would open the floor to questions, staying until the last question was asked and answered.

He always prefaced the session with a caveat, which I paraphrase here: "When you ask a question, I will give you one of three responses. First, if I know the answer and can give it to you, I will. Second, if I don't know the answer, I promise to find the answer and get it to you.

(continued on next page)

Third, there may be some sensitive areas, such as a pending industry partnership or pending litigation, where the answer is too sensitive to reveal at this time. In that case, I will tell you that I cannot give you the answer, and I will promise to provide the answer as soon as it no longer threatens the company's interests."

He kept his word. Sometimes the session went on for an hour, and others reached almost four hours. There were times when the "question" was more of a statement, but he always listened and learned.

When leaders or employees at any level take the time to teach, they find that they also learn a lot through the experience. Your own understanding of a subject generally increases as you organize your thoughts and really think about how best to present the information. Preparing for teaching forces you to reflect on what you know.

If you have never taught a class or presented at a conference, I encourage you to do so. Besides learning from your audience, you can also "learn from yourself." When you are planning a lecture, you are forced to think about what you want to impart to your audience or

---

Teach to Learn

Throughout my career as a corporate training manager, consultant, and author, I have focused on planning and developing training programs. Rarely have I passed up any opportunity to teach, whether inside the company, as a workshop leader, a conference presenter, or an adjunct college professor. I always seem to learn more from my students than I teach them. For the past five years, I have taught courses on organization development, teamwork, and leadership to adult learners in a master's-degree program in management at a Boston-area college. At the start of each class, I tell the students that they have as much to teach me as I have to teach them. Although I have more than 20 years of experience in the business world, collectively they have more than 150 years of experience! They have much to teach each other and me.

your students. This process, in and of itself, can provide tremendous value to you in identifying the tacit knowledge that you want to share.

At the same time, leaders who teach also find that they can learn a lot from their audiences. At one time, in planning a sales-training event, I asked several engineers to act as teachers. Their response was not enthusiastic: "You want us to talk to *salespeople?* What value can there be to us from talking with *them?*"

At the first of these sales-training events, I had to "force" the engineers to make the presentations by calling in chips from some of their managers. Once they did their sessions, their tune changed: "You know, I actually learned something from those people!" In fact, the word got around that there was real value in making these presentations; after all, the salespeople had much closer contact with customers than did the engineers, and they knew more about how customers were actually using the products, what customers wanted for new features, and so forth. At the next sales-training sessions, many engineers volunteered to give presentations.

Building an Organization-Wide Infrastructure for Learning

When I talk about building an infrastructure for learning, I refer to a broad spectrum of changes that can be made to encourage employee learning, sharing of ideas and knowledge, and the application of knowledge, skills, and ideas to help achieve individual, group, and company goals. These modifications may include the following:

- changes in organizational design
- changes in physical plant
- changes in measurement and reward systems
- changes in policies and procedures
- changes in the training organization
- changes in technology and communications infrastructures.

Changes in Organizational Design

Does the design of your organization encourage or hinder learning? *good question* Does the design enable people to share knowledge and ideas or bar them from doing so? Are groups so "stove-piped" that communications between groups cannot happen except at the top of the organization?

Is cross-functional teamwork widespread, or is it the exception to the rule?

Although no one organizational design is perfect for every company or for every learning opportunity, poor organizational design can inhibit or even bar the sharing of knowledge and ideas. Leaders in the company should start the examination of organizational design at the top levels: How common is cross-functional, cross-business unit teamwork among the company's top officers? If it does not exist at that level, it almost certainly won't exist at lower levels. Lead by example—show the rest of the company what needs to be done and make your own cross-functional learning experiences a benchmark for groups and individuals at all levels of the company.

WMAT

Changes in Physical Plant

Does the design of your physical plant encourage or inhibit learning and the sharing of ideas? One company invested a great deal of money in building a learning center at its main manufacturing plant. The learning center included workstations for taking multimedia and CBT programs, a large video library with small carrels equipped with videocassette players, a lending library of books and tapes, counseling rooms where employees could meet with learning advisors, and other commendable features and programs. But the plant was massive, and the learning center was located at one end, so that it was a 10-minute walk for many employees—too far for someone to drop in during lunch break. Its location was remote from the parking area, so that people were discouraged from dropping in at the beginning or end of the workday because of the extra time it would take. The solution was to create smaller learning centers scattered throughout the plant.

In many manufacturing plants, small, soundproof conference rooms have been built throughout the noisy manufacturing areas to enable and encourage employees to meet together to exchange ideas and learn from each other. Before the conference rooms were built, communication among employees was nearly impossible; because of the noise levels, the employees literally had to shout to be heard.

Of course, changes in plant design won't make any difference at all if the company doesn't have a PLE. Several companies have tried these and other innovations in plant design but have not been successful in improving learning on the job because the company's

attitude was, "We're paying you to work, not to talk with each other."
In other companies, management decided to minimize the number of
conference rooms because "employees should spend their time working, not wasting time in meetings." From my point of view, if employees are wasting time in meetings, it is mostly a sign of poor leadership
and poor meeting planning; properly planned and executed meetings
can be prime learning opportunities for all involved.

Changes in Measurement and Reward Systems

One of the primary reasons why most corporate change efforts
don't work is that the leaders tell employees that they want them to
change, yet the company continues to measure and reward them for
doing things in the same old ways. If you want the movement to ISDL
to work, to make a real contribution to the company's bottom line,
you must realign measurement and reward systems to make it clear
that learning is important. Successful companies have done this in
many ways, including the following:

- *Pay for learning*. Some companies offer monetary incentives
  to employees who acquire new skills. These companies have
  formal competency profiles for employees and wage increases
  that are tied to the numbers of competencies achieved. This is
  more common in industrial companies and especially with
  factory workers, less so with white-collar industries and jobs.

- *Reward learning champions*. In companies with a strong
  learning environment, rewards are given to employees who
  help others learn by teaching a class, by being a coach or mentor, by contributing to online discussions, and so on. Rewards
  are also given to employees who seek new knowledge and
  skills by asking questions, volunteering for learning-related
  assignments, and the like, and who then apply their learning to
  their jobs to affect company results in a positive way.

- *Make learning a job requirement*. In many forward-looking
  companies, learning is a required part of every employee's job
  plan. Although many companies include a section on employee development in the annual performance or salary review
  process, these sections are in many cases pointless because no
  measurements or rewards are attached to them. In companies

that take learning seriously, up to 25 percent of salary increases are based on meeting learning objectives. A learning contract (figure 4-1) can provide a model for employee-development plans.

- *Recognize learning achievements*. Recognition for learning achievements can be even more important than monetary rewards. By publicizing learning achievements, company leaders make it known that they place value on learning activities. For example, at Wang Global in Canada, employees who achieve a professional certification, such as MCSE, are given a specially embroidered shirt that has both the Wang Global logo and the MCSE logo. More important, the shirts are presented at a public ceremony during which top managers celebrate the employee's achievement.

What I am talking about here is developing a company culture that encourages employees to learn. Too often, company leaders pay lip service to learning activities while sending implicit, but clearly heard messages that people shouldn't waste their own or the company's time on learning activities.

Changes in Policies and Procedures

Many companies' policies and procedures mandate the ways in which people must do their work, leaving no room for change or improvement. Perhaps the original intent of these policies and procedures might have been to standardize work procedures to ensure a consistently good product or service, but they become outdated. Work continues to be done according to the outdated policies and procedures because "that's what it says in the book."

If you want people to learn and to apply their learning to their work to make a positive difference in individual, group, and corporate business results, you cannot allow policies and procedures to tie employees' hands. The phrase, "because we've always done it that way," has ruined many chances for improvement in almost every company.

Standardized policies and procedures are also designed to protect the company from litigation. Legal departments examine policies and procedures to ensure that they mandate legal, nondiscriminatory practices within the company. In today's litigious society, this is a real concern for most companies. At the same time, legal caution can sometimes go too far. For example, at one company that was trying to encourage employees to gain an industry certification, the training group wrote a manager's guide. The guide suggested that managers encourage their employees to sign up for training and then continue to encourage them through the training and certification process, all of which was being done via ISDL. When the company's legal staff reviewed this guidebook, they added several introductory paragraphs, warning managers to be careful what they said to employees. Basically, what the lawyers told managers was that they could tell employees that getting certified was good for their careers and that getting certified was good for the company, but they were not allowed to tell them that getting certified "was good for their careers at the company." This latter statement, said the lawyers, might imply a commitment to continued employment on the part of the company and, should it become necessary to fire or lay off an employee, the employee could sue the company on the basis of this implied commitment. No doubt it is the job of the legal department to protect the company's interests, but it is up to the leaders of the company to determine exactly what is and what isn't in the company's best interests and to ensure that the right messages are getting through to employees. Employees who are in constant fear of losing their jobs won't have the best motivation for ISDL unless they see it as a method of getting a better job somewhere else.

Changes in the Training Organization

If the movement to ISDL is to succeed in a company, the mission, role, and behaviors of the training organization are going to have to change dramatically. Rather than being the sole source for properly designed and delivered training programs, the training group will have to assume the role of learning facilitation—a major transformation for most traditional training groups. Learning Facilitator my title (ideally

When company leaders mandate the change to ISDL, it is often with the idea of eliminating or greatly reducing the size of the company's training group. I believe that this is a grave error. But to survive, if not to thrive, the training group will have to redefine itself and acquire new skills and methods. These will be discussed at greater length in chapter 6.

Changes in the Technology and Communications Infrastructure

Today's technology can ease the way to ISDL in a variety of ways. At the same time, remember that technology does not *cause* change. *People* make change happen. Technology can enable change—it can make it possible. Technology can facilitate change—it can make it easier. But technology cannot cause change—it cannot make it happen. The role of technology infrastructure in ISDL will be discussed in chapters 7 and 8.

LEARNING ASSIGNMENT

Do your company's leaders walk the learning talk? Create a plan for the company's top officers, starting with the CEO, to communicate the importance of employee learning by demonstrating their personal commitment to their own learning and the learning activities of other employees. Use ideas in the following checklists to help you develop a plan.

Leaders' Learning Checklist

To be an effective leader for learning, company leaders must first recognize how they themselves learn and then develop ways to demonstrate their own learning activities to company employees. Do your company leaders use any of the following ways to learn?

❏ holding discussions with customers

❏ attending trade shows

❏ attending an industry conference

❏ reading books and articles

(continued on next page)

Leaders' Learning Checklist *(continued)*

❏ meeting with consultants or academics
❏ holding discussions with the company's board of directors
❏ holding discussions with their own staffs, individually or in groups
❏ meeting with employees.

Can you think of other means used by your company's leaders for learning?

How Leaders Make Their Learning Visible to Employees

How many of the following ways do your company leaders use to make their own learning activities visible to employees?

❏ holding open meetings with employees where they talk about what they have learned

❏ participating in employee discussion forums on the company's intranet

❏ writing a column in the company's employee newsletter

❏ raising new ideas from their learning in board meetings, in staff meetings, and in one-to-one meetings with employees

❏ sharing a recently read book or article with employees and setting up a time to discuss the ideas it raised.

Can you think of other means that your company leaders use?

ENDNOTE

* From Tom Brown, "MG—The New Ideas Website," by permission of the author. (1999). http://www.mgeneral.com/1-lines/98-lines/-0221981i.htm.

Chapter 6

Redefining Corporate Training

When the CEO tells the company's training group that the company will move to ISDL as the primary mode of learning, how does the training group typically react? Training groups in this situation generally adopt one of four strategies:

- *Strategy 1:* The training group argues against the change.
- *Strategy 2:* The training group ignores the mandate.
- *Strategy 3:* The training group immediately abandons its traditional role and moves everything into a self-paced format.
- *Strategy 4:* The training group works with corporate leadership to find the right balance of traditional training methods and newer, self-paced training methods, leading the change effort to benefit the company and its employees.

The first two of these strategies are not productive and will only lead to the faster demise of the corporate training function for reasons outlined later in the chapter. The third strategy is equally unproductive for the training group, the company, and the employees. The last strategy is the one I strongly recommend. Let's examine each of the strategies in turn.

STRATEGY 1: ARGUING AGAINST THE MANDATE

The training profession, like many other professions, often gets trapped in its own paradigms. Graduate schools and the many publicly available training programs for training professionals teach that there is one right way to develop and deliver training—the so-called scientific method. To stray from "the right way" would seem to violate the standards and vocational pride of training professionals. To avoid such violations, training professionals may reject corporate mandates, ISDL among them, which would cause them seemingly to violate those standards. After all, one of the classic definitions of a professional is a person who pays more allegiance to the standards of the profession than to the needs of his or her employer.

I have seen training managers argue against the movement to ISDL to the point where I worried about their blood pressure. I have seen other training managers resign on the spot rather than "betray the profession." I have heard others tell their corporate leadership exactly what they think of the new mandate to the point of being fired. None of these is a winning strategy for the training manager, for the training group, for the company, or for the employees.

The wiser training manager discusses the mandate with corporate leadership to discover the reasons behind the mandate (almost always, cost is at the top of the list) and negotiates with management to find a path that will help meet the corporate mandate while preserving the professionalism of the training group. This will be discussed at greater length under strategy 4.

STRATEGY 2: IGNORING THE MANDATE

In some companies, the training function is zero-budgeted, that is, it receives no corporate funding but recovers its costs by charging tuition to people attending its programs. If the mandate to move to ISDL is imposed on this type of training group but corporate leadership does nothing to change departmental training budgets, the training group may believe that it can ignore the corporate mandate. After all, its "real customers" still want to come to training and are willing to pay for it. The training group may reduce the number of programs it offers in corporate facilities to make its work less visible and do more training at remote locations, but basically the group is still ignoring the corporate mandate.

Again, this strategy may postpone the inevitable reduction in the size and scope of the training group, but it will not avoid it altogether. The corporate leaders who imposed the mandate did so because they realized how much the company was spending on training and training-related activities (travel, expenses, time off the job, and so forth) and wanted to reduce that amount. At some point in the future, they will examine those numbers again and, seeing little or no reduction in costs, will come down even harder on the training group for having ignored their mandate. The outcome in that case can be more drastic: the group may be eliminated totally or the training function may be outsourced.

STRATEGY 3: ACCEDING TO THE MANDATE

Some training groups react to the mandate to move to ISDL by "giving them what they want." They rush headlong to convert everything they do into a self-paced format, to purchase packaged programs from external suppliers, to convert training materials into hypertext markup language (HTML) format, and put them all on a Website. I have seen companies that have consolidated all of their product documentation into a Website and call it self-paced training. I have also seen many suppliers rushing to fill the market with self-paced training materials to meet the growing demand and cash in on the trend to self-directed learning, only to produce overpriced programs that are all but useless.

The Rush to Market

With the unstoppable movement toward ISDL, suppliers have rushed to market with an incredible array of products described as self-paced training—Web-based training, CD-ROM, videotapes, distance-learning programs, and many more. It seems that anyone who has a PC, some tools to create multimedia instructional programs, and a desire to

(continued on next page)

The Rush to Market *(continued)*

cash in on the trend is producing and marketing an astounding variety of programs. As a corporate-training manager, I get several telephone calls a day and dozens of direct mail advertisements every week for such products.

Caveat emptor—let the buyer beware! I find it hard to believe that I have wasted my time reviewing some of this junk. For example, I looked at one CD-ROM training program that painted the screen with words, with voice-over narration reading the words. This was repeated for approximately 200 screens. The type was about 12 point in size, graphics were nonexistent, and color was totally lacking (both on the screens and in the narrator's voice). In some cases, the word-wraps were wrong; in other cases, the words ran off the screen with no scroll bar to capture all of the text. At $395 per copy, it would have been much less expensive and much more effective to give employees a book on the subject.

In another Web-based training program that I previewed from a vendor's Website, the graphics were spectacular. I had never seen such a beautiful program. But, the graphics were so detailed, the effects so spectacular, the motion so smooth, that the file sizes caused great delays in downloading the images. The show was fun to watch, but the special effects had little to do with the content and, therefore, added no value.

I watched the first 10 minutes of an "instructional" videotape from a renowned expert that was nothing but a headshot of a person lecturing from notes. The total training program included eight hour-long videotapes. I wasn't about to spend eight hours watching this disembodied head talk to me.

Many outstanding self-paced training programs and learning resources are available on the market today. But, as with any trend, many who are sometimes unscrupulous, sometimes ill-prepared are trying to cash in on the movement to ISDL with little regard for the quality of their products. Don't buy anything unless you preview it and several competing products.

Putting everything into a self-paced format, eliminating instructor-led training, creating lots of CD-ROMs and Web-based learning materials cannot guarantee that employees will learn what they need to improve their job performance. Of course, the great majority of corporate-training expense is already being wasted, because it is not tied to specific business objectives of the company (Tobin 1997). Will the move to ISDL help improve the company's ROI for training? Logically, it should help. In the most simplistic terms, ROI is the ratio of benefits to costs:

$$ROI = \frac{B}{C}$$

If costs (C) decrease, the value of the ratio increases. Although it is always important to control costs, I believe it is much more important to focus on the benefit (B) side of the ratio. If the training offered by the training group offers little benefit to the company and its employees in terms of meeting their business objectives, a reduction in costs may improve the ratio, but business goals will go unmet. Merely acceding to a corporate mandate to convert everything to ISDL will do nothing to increase the value of B and may, in fact, lessen the value of B if it is not done in a judicious manner, as described in strategy 4.

STRATEGY 4: FINDING THE RIGHT BALANCE

There is much to commend the movement to ISDL—for some topics and for some audiences. Not every topic lends itself to this approach, nor is ISDL the right delivery method for some audiences. Even where the topic is appropriate for ISDL and the delivery method matches the audience's learning style, it behooves the training group to work with the target audience to ensure that employees know how best to use the new approach to meet their learning needs. To make this movement work best for a company, the training group should examine

- which topics lend themselves to ISDL and which require other learning methods
- which audiences can benefit most from ISDL and which will not benefit from the new approach
- how the training group can help employees use the new learning methods.

Choosing Topics for ISDL

To determine whether ISDL is the right solution to a learning problem or whether a traditional training program should be converted to an ISDL format, you must consider several issues to ensure a good fit between business objectives and employee-learning goals. Here, I present the "Top 10 Questions to Ask When Choosing ISDL" to help you cover all the bases. I will address each of these questions in the subsections that follow.

Top 10 Questions to Ask When Choosing ISDL

1. Is any type of training or learning activity really going to solve the problem the company is facing?

2. Can the needed topics of instruction be defined for the vast majority of the target audience or will the success of the learning activity greatly depend on the ability of an instructor to adapt the content to audience needs in real time?

3. How much value comes from the personal interaction of the participants with an instructor or with other members of the class?

4. How much hands-on experience is required for the employee to master the learning content, that is, to take the information and turn it into personal knowledge?

5. What is the size of the target audience?

6. What is the cost of creating ISDL versus using traditional, instructor-led training methods?

7. How quickly does the training need to be done? How long will its value last before it has to be redone or before it is abandoned?

8. Is technology available to support learning activities? How accessible is that technology to your target audience?

9. Which resources are available to reinforce learning as employees take an ISDL course and later as they apply their learning to their work?

10. How will the target audience respond to ISDL? What if you did no training of any type? How would people learn what they needed?

Question 1. Before even asking the question as to whether ISDL is the right training method, a more basic question must be asked: Is training/learning the right solution to the problem? Too many times, training groups (and company leaders) rush to implement a training solution when the problem relates to something else and no training program, no matter how good, will solve the problem. For example, if a plant's machinery is just worn out, no amount of training on using that equipment will bring it back to life. Or, if the rewards for the sales-force are tied directly and solely to the sale of product or service *A,* no amount of training on product or service *B* will induce a sales-person to sell it. As is too often the case, a company leader will ask the training group to develop a training program and because that is what the training group does, it will accept the job even though the training will never solve the initial problem.

Question 2. What is the nature of the content of the training/learning? Can the needed topic of instruction be defined for the vast majority of the target audience or will the success of the learning activity greatly depend on the ability of an instructor to adapt the content to audience needs in real time?

Ideally, a topic for ISDL will be a fixed body of knowledge, which, if it changes at all, changes only slightly over time. For example, the principles of electronics remain relatively constant. If your company has adopted a new, electronic-spreadsheet system for companywide use, the topic is well defined, and basic features probably won't change for a few years. On the opposite end of the spectrum, an ISDL program that teaches salespeople about the company's competitors and their products and services will probably have a very short shelf-life, especially in very competitive industries, such as high technology or biotechnology.

For a new, company-standard spreadsheet, email, or word-processing program, the needs of the audience can be defined ahead of time. Different levels of instruction may be needed. For example, accountants and finance professionals may need more advanced training than line managers on new spreadsheet features and functions, but these can be defined ahead of time.

On the other hand, there are topics for which the employees' questions cannot be fully anticipated and where getting answers to specific questions is what employees are seeking. For example, you might be able to teach the basic procedures for your company's new, employee-performance rating system via ISDL, but managers who attend are going to have specific questions about the employees they manage. This is where ISDL cannot equal or even approach the value of a live instructor.

Question 3. How much value comes from the personal interaction of the participants with an instructor or with other participants? Over the course of my career, I have developed 100 or more learning activities, courses, symposia, and workshops. I have always firmly believed that more than half the value to the participants in these programs has come not from the program content itself, but from the informal interaction of the participants with the instructors and other participants. There are many ways of enabling and facilitating these types of interactions electronically, but the electronic methods don't provide, and probably never will, the intimacy of personal conversations. Electronic methods also make it more difficult to maintain anonymity; if you are dealing with a sensitive situation, it is one thing to have a one-on-one conversation with an instructor or colleague but a totally different matter to publicize your situation in a chat room or on an electronic bulletin board.

Question 4. How much hands-on experience is required for the employee to master the knowledge or skill and apply it to his or her job? You can simulate many kinds of hands-on experience via electronic means, but it is very difficult to duplicate it. Annapolis-based Mentor Technologies has created a series of laboratory exercises that enable people to do laboratory exercises on live, Cisco-networking equipment over an Internet link. These exercises can be very useful to people who are preparing to take Cisco's technical-certification examinations. At the same time, put yourself in the shoes of a customer. Would you want a technician to come into your place of business to install a new Cisco network who has never seen or laid hands on a piece of Cisco equipment?

Question 5. What is the size of your target audience? How geographically dispersed is that audience? Even with the latest in low-cost, easy-to-use development tools, substantial costs are involved in developing, testing, and deploying ISDL. Generally, the larger the audience for any ISDL program, the more you can afford to invest in its development. Similarly, the more geographically dispersed the audience, the more it will cost to use traditional training methods. You either have to convene the audience at a central site or send instructors out to the field; both options tend to make ISDL more cost-effective than instructor-led training.

Question 6. What is the cost of creating ISDL versus using traditional stand-up training methods? Compare the costs of ISDL versus traditional training methods. Some time ago, I received an email message from a person in a company's IS organization. The IS group was about to implement a new asset management system that it had purchased from an outside supplier. The supplier had recommended yet another company to create a Web-based training program on the system. "This supplier is asking $300,000 to create the training program. Does that sound reasonable?" was the query.

My response was to ask many questions, starting with the following:

- How many people need to be trained and where are those people located?

- How intuitive is the new asset management system? Are there "help" features or a tutorial built into it?

- What does the audience need to learn?

- What alternatives have you considered for training delivery and in terms of alternative suppliers?

- The only immediate advice I could offer was, "Don't sign a contract with this supplier until we discuss these and other questions." Too many times, because ISDL is the current "method of choice" for corporate training, people rush into it headlong without asking basic, necessary questions.

Question 7. How quickly does the training need to be done? How long will its value last before it has to be redone or before it is abandoned? These are important questions. Just like traditional, instructor-led training, ISDL takes time to develop. Some methods take more time than others. Also, some ISDL methods are easier to update than others; Web-based training, for example, can be updated much more easily than a CD-ROM-based program, because you have to track down and replace all existing CDs if you want people to use the latest version of a program. Similarly, lead times vary according to the ISDL methodology and tools selected.

Question 8. What technology is available to support employee-learning activities? This is a vital question. To create a CD-ROM-based program doesn't make sense if few employees have CD-ROMs on their personal computers. Web-based training makes little sense if employees don't have personal computers or if they don't have Web access. Even if these capabilities can be provided in special learning centers at each of the company's locations, these training strategies won't make sense for a program that must be taken by all employees in a short period of time. You need to make certain that employees have the capability of using the ISDL methods you are propagating.

Question 9. What resources are available to reinforce learning as employees take an ISDL course and later as they apply their learning to their work? It is one thing to be able to say that X number of employees have completed an ISDL program. It is a very different thing to say that X number of employees have applied what they learned to their work with specific job objectives being achieved as a result.

If an employee is taking an ISDL program and doesn't understand the material or has a question, who will answer those questions or provide additional help? These questions have to be answered as part of your ISDL strategy if you want to be truly successful in implementing ISDL. To paraphrase technology and learning guru Elliott Masie, in a classroom setting, an employee will sit through a boring lecture and wait until he or she can ask a question to clarify something he or she doesn't understand. With a technology-based learning program, as soon as the employee finds the material unclear or has a question that he or she cannot ask, "leaving the program takes just one click of the mouse." Learners have much lower tolerance for poor instruction from an ISDL program than they do in a live classroom situation.

Question 10. How will ISDL be received by the target audience? Without training, how would people learn what they need to learn? People learn every day as part of their jobs with no intervention from the training group. They are ingenious in finding ways to learn what they need to get their jobs done. You should always consider the option of no training at all. Perhaps a job aid might fulfill the employees' needs. Perhaps you can train a small cadre of technical personnel at the company's major locations with the goal that they then provide informal instruction to local employees. There are many nontraining strategies that should be considered to meet any learning need. As stated in the discussion around question 1, training isn't always the right solution.

Determining the Best Audience for ISDL

Several instruments on the market, called "learning styles inventories," focus on the ways in which people prefer to learn—listening, reading, doing, and so forth. The field of neurolinguistic programming (NLP) also focuses on individual learning styles. An in-depth discussion of learning styles is beyond the scope of this book, but it is important for the training group to remember that not everyone can learn best from a single method of instruction.

My current company has invested heavily in CBT for technical education. Although most of our employees seem satisfied with this method of training, there are many exceptions. For example, we heard from one employee who is dyslexic and cannot learn by reading text on a computer screen. Two employees in Singapore spent the four hours they spent commuting on the train every day studying together from books and achieved their technical certifications in a very short time. Other employees are barred from using CBT because they work inside secure government facilities and cannot penetrate the firewall to access our Website where the courseware resides. With the exception of the employee with dyslexia, these other employees could have used the CBT courses, but they had either chosen not to or had encountered some barrier to their use.

Whether or not you choose to test every employee to determine learning style preferences, you must realize that ISDL comes in many forms, and some will be better suited to some employees than to others. You must also recognize that just because some company has put a course on videotape, on a CD-ROM, or on a Website doesn't mean that that method is the best way to present the material or that it is automatically a good program. For example:

Some years ago, I designed and produced a three-day seminar for one of my clients. The client suggested that we videotape the seminar and make the tapes available to a wider audience within the company. They abandoned the idea when I asked them who would sit and watch 24 hours of videotape. With today's technology, we could have reached a larger audience by broadcasting the seminar via teleconference or, using some of the more modern computer-conferencing capabilities, over the company's intranet. The latter approach could have added the capability to ask questions. All participants, even those several thousand miles away, could have been part of the live audience.

Not everyone likes CBT. If you sit at a computer all day long, do you really want to go home and use a CBT program that requires that you stare at it for more several more hours? Some people have much more tolerance for staring at the monitor than others.

Some people find more value from the live interaction of a classroom, no matter what the subject matter, than from any type of self-paced material. They need an instructor to lead them through the material and other people with whom to interact to test their own understanding of the material.

Some subjects demand hands-on experience. You don't want to learn how to paint a picture or repair a computer exclusively from a book or video—you need to get your hands dirty to see how it really works.

When selecting an ISDL method, there are other basic considerations that you have to take into account. For example, Web-based training assumes that every employee in your target population has Web access. At Wang Global, even though we are a well-networked company, we ran into firewall problems for employees who worked in some government and commercial customer facilities. You also have to consider access speeds. The telecommunications infrastructure in some countries is so weak that downloading a CBT program from a network-based server is impractical at best.

When using video- or computer-conferencing, you need to take into account time-zone differences, so that you are not forcing some employees to attend training at 3:00 in the morning. If you are providing videotapes to employees, you should make certain that their local offices have videocassette players and monitors available to view those tapes. If you are providing tapes internationally, you have to check on the standards for recording and viewing such tapes.

Before rushing to convert a traditional program to ISDL or before choosing ISDL as the medium for delivering a new program, examine your audience and the subject matter. Choose a method, or a variety of methods, that will help you achieve the company's business objectives, as well as the individual's learning objectives. Clearly, ISDL has a lot to offer, but it is not always the right answer.

Helping Employees Use ISDL

Despite the popularity of the movie *Field of Dreams,* it isn't necessarily true that "if you build it, they will come." If employees have become dependent on the company's training group to tell them what training they need and to provide instructor-led training on any and all subjects, a sudden decree telling them that they must now determine their own learning needs and study on their own won't immediately be met with great enthusiasm.

Some employees will resent the withdrawal of support from the training group and will refuse to have anything more to do with it. Some employees will find the new learning methods unsatisfying and will stop taking programs. Still other employees will turn outside the company to find programs based upon the old methods with which they are comfortable. Unfortunately, some employees may even leave the company to find another employer who will give them training in the old way. Some employees will pay lip-service to the new methods, but will not take training because they lack the equipment needed for the program.

In other words, you can't make the switch to ISDL and expect that everyone will enthusiastically welcome the change and immediately start using the new learning methods. You need to *sell* ISDL from the top of the organization to the bottom. You need to build a whole new learning culture within the company, and this will be the subject of chapter 9.

NEW ROLES FOR THE TRAINING ORGANIZATION

There are five roles that the corporate training organization should play if ISDL is to succeed in your company:

- developing and delivering training courses and materials, whether those are self-paced or more traditional, instructor-led training
- teaching employees at all levels to identify their own learning needs
- researching and publishing learning guides
- coaching employees to identify and use learning resources
- teaching knowledge-resource people how to share their knowledge.

The first role is already familiar to the training group. The four additional roles, which are the subject of the next few subsections, are likely to be new for most training groups.

Teaching Employees to Identify Their Own Learning Needs

If ISDL is to succeed in any organization, employees at all levels must learn how to identify their own learning needs. In many companies where traditional training groups have long offered a large catalog of courses, employees have become so dependent on the training group that they will be at a loss to identify their own learning needs without that catalog. The learning contract (figure 4-1) is one primary means of having the employee, in conjunction with his or her manager, identify what needs to be learned to help meet individual, group, and corporate goals. The process of developing a learning contract is new to most employees and to their managers, as well. They need to learn how to translate corporate business goals into individual learning objectives, and it is the training group that should take responsibility for ensuring that this learning occurs.

The next question is, "Which instructional methods should be used to teach employees to identify their own learning needs?" With the push for ISDL, many organizations have jumped at the opportunity to teach these skills in a self-paced format, whether through a Web-based, CD-ROM, or paper-based program. I believe that this is a mistake; if employees are not comfortable with ISDL, you shouldn't expect them to learn about it from ISDL. One of the lessons we learned at Wang Global was that employees who don't spend time surfing the Web weren't going to learn about our Web-based programs through our intranet Website. We needed to use a lot of print materials to publicize the Website for the many employees who wouldn't find the Website on their own. Similarly, I believe that you need to start the push to ISDL through live, instructor-led workshops to familiarize employees with the new methods and materials and provide them with some level of comfort with the new learning methods.

Researching and Publishing Learning Guides

Even while we are asking employees to take responsibility for their own learning, if we want ISDL to succeed, we need to make the job easy for them. A major role that the training group can play in this regard is to research and publish learning guides.

Learning guides are much easier to develop if the company has a set of competency profiles in place for all jobs. When competency profiles exist, you can simply attach lists of learning resources to each competency as has been done at the Dow Chemical Company and at the Canadian Imperial Bank of Commerce. If your company does not have such profiles, you can still develop learning guides keyed to specific areas of knowledge and skills. For each knowledge or skill area, you should list:

- *Internal courses:* instructor-led, self-paced, Web-based, and so forth

- *External courses:* college courses, distance-learning courses, self-paced materials available from various professional groups and suppliers, courses provided by professional and industry organizations, consultants, and training groups

- *Bibliography:* listing of books, videotapes, audiotapes, CD-ROMs, articles, and other resources on the topic

- *Other publications:* magazines, professional journals, and newsletters related to the topic

- *Electronic resources:* Websites (internal and external), listserv discussions, "communities of practice" sites

- *Knowledge-network resources:* from inside and outside the company, as will be described more fully in chapter 8.

Some training groups have balked at the idea of publishing learning guides: "Why should we be sending people to other courses and giving them alternative ways of learning when we have courses in our own catalog that will meet their needs? We'll just be putting ourselves out of business!" These groups have to realize that their world is changing and that they will have to change their roles from training-only providers to learning facilitators—a reflection of the fact that learning encompasses much more than a traditional training catalog.

Coaching Employees

Providing learning guides for employees is a necessary first step, but to make ISDL really work, the training group will have to coach employees on how to use those learning guides to identify their learning needs, find the right learning resources to meet those needs, and use those resources in the best way. Even when you hold workshops for employees, many will still need coaching to effectively use the new learning strategies and methods that have been described in the workshop. Some companies, such as the Canadian Imperial Bank of Commerce, have developed a team of learning counselors to coach employees.

Ideally, when an employee learns a new subject and is ready to try it out on the job, the employee's manager should act as a coach. This presumes that the manager knows the subject matter and that the man-

---

Coaching Each Other at Wang Global

At Wang Global, we continuously receive telephone calls and email messages from employees who want to know if we provide training on a given topic. We respond to each call. If we don't have a training program in place on the topic, we do research on available learning resources (books, Websites, external training programs, and so forth) and give the employee as many learning alternatives as possible. We also post all of this research on our internal Website so that others can use the research should they have a similar learning need. Posting these queries on the Website also allows employees to coach each other by discussing how they have learned a subject or by telling of learning resources they have discovered on various topics.

All Learning Is Self-Directed

ager has good coaching skills. One of the most common errors made in companies today is that they tell managers, "We are going to require your employees to do their work in a new and different manner. Because the change won't be easy, we need you to coach your employees to ensure that they get it right and master the new skills." The idea of turning managers into coaches is a good one. Nevertheless, few companies recognize that the role of manager as coach is a new one for managers and that the managers need to learn and master these new skills just as their employees need to learn and master their new skills. Most companies assume that managers can learn quickly these new coaching skills on their own and provide them with little or no training and little or no coaching for themselves. One of the most valuable functions of the training group is training managers on coaching skills and then coaching managers as they try out these new skills.

Teaching Knowledge-Resource People How to Share Their Knowledge

People don't just learn from classes and educational materials. A primary means of employee learning is learning from other people. This is how tacit knowledge—knowledge that cannot be easily written down—is usually shared. A knowledge network, as will be described in chapter 8, helps employees make connections with people who have knowledge and skills that they need to acquire.

Still, sharing knowledge is not as easy as it sounds. Your company's most important knowledge resources are known as key resources because their knowledge is valued, and they are busy doing what they do to help the company. A vital role that the training group can play is in helping these key people find ways to share their knowledge with others while minimizing the effect on their regular work.

How can you help the company's knowledge resources share their knowledge, both explicit and tacit, with other employees who need to build their own knowledge and skills? Of the myriad ways available, some are easier than others. The following methods can be used to transfer explicit knowledge:

- Have the employee teach a class.
- Have the employee write a manual.
- Have the employee make an audio- or videotape recording.
- Ask the employee to allow others to shadow him/her
- Ask the employee to intentionally mentor others
   coach

Sharing Knowledge Through Expert Systems

A large oil company had one employee who was the world's leading expert on reading seismic graphs to determine the probability that there was an underground oil deposit. This person was nearing retirement age, and the company didn't want to lose the benefit of the knowledge and the wisdom he had accumulated over the years. The company's solution was to create an expert system—an artificial-intelligence application that would mimic the employee's thought processes in reading and interpreting seismic graphs.

The company assigned an expert on artificial intelligence to spend six months working with the employee to develop a rules-based expert system that would mimic the employee's thought processes. At the end of six months, the new system was introduced and it was good, very good. In fact, it reached the 80 to 85 percent level of the employee's expertise. Nevertheless, during the process of creating the artificial-intelligence program, the programmer became the world's second-leading expert on reading seismic graphs.

The moral of this story is that some categories of knowledge and skills can never be made explicit but must remain tacit. At the same time, this tacit knowledge can be transmitted from one person to another through dialogue and demonstration.

Often when an employee is asked to help with training in one of these ways, he or she responds, "I don't have time to do training. I have real work to do. Why doesn't the training department take care of it—it's their job, not mine." This type of response reflects the lack of a PLE. In a PLE, every employee is open to sharing his or her knowledge with others.

I once faced this type of problem with a brilliant engineer who, in response to my request to put together a training session, said, "I don't have time to develop anything formal. Just put me in a room with the people you want to train, and I'll do it off the top of my head. They'll get what they need, and I won't have to spend a lot of time preparing." The problem with this solution was that the engineer was known for being a disorganized presenter and for the illegibility of his drawings. I asked him if he would be willing to give the session twice with a few weeks between the sessions. He agreed.

To solve the problem, I selected three people from the target audience—a near-expert, a fairly experienced person, and a neophyte—plus an instructional developer, a graphics designer, and a court stenographer to be in the audience for his first session. The instructional designer was there to help structure the presentation, not to interrupt him while he was presenting, but to help structure the presentation for the second session. The intention was for the graphics designer to copy down the drawings that he made on the white board and, later, to develop a better set of visual aids. The court stenographer was there to capture the presentation verbatim.

The three people from the target audience were key to the effort. They were there to ensure that the engineer's presentation met the needs of the target audience, in this case field-support people. Without their presence, the engineer would have presented what *he* thought they needed to know, rather than what *they* thought they needed to know.

At the conclusion of the presentation, the instructional designer developed a detailed outline for the second session and worked with the graphics designer to develop a series of legible slides for the engineer. The engineer was delighted to have both the outline and the slides. At the second session, we created a videotape that we then distributed to a large, widely scattered field audience. The result was that we were able to meet the learning needs of about 200 field-support people in 20 or more countries at a minimal cost and with a minimum investment of time from this important engineer. We followed up the training by using the company's discussion forums (as will be described in chapter 8) so that follow-up questions could be answered.

This happened about 15 years ago. Today, we might use a videoconference or a computer-based conference to achieve the same end. Properly preparing for making the videotape and ensuring that it met the needs of the target audience were fundamental to the success of the learning activity. Similar preparations will add equal value to the planning of more up-to-date delivery methods.

THE NEW TRAINING ORGANIZATION

Whether or not your company has mandated the change to ISDL, the types of analysis and changes described in this chapter can be of great benefit to traditional training organizations. Certainly, traditional training activities should not be totally abandoned in any company. In the future of corporate training and development, ISDL has an important role to play, and every corporate-training group ought to consider the myriad alternatives to formal, instructor-led training that are available in today's market and with today's technology.

These changes will not be easy for many traditional training groups, which have done the same things the same ways for so many years, especially if they have been successful with the traditional methods of instructional design and delivery. Just as virtually every part of today's corporation is being asked to change the ways that they have traditionally worked, just as training groups have been asked to help the other parts of their companies to learn and adapt to the necessary changes, so also must the learning needs of the training group itself be addressed.

Too often, the training group is so involved in preparing others for change that it forgets that it needs to help itself. For example, over the past 10 to 15 years, I have seen dozens of articles in the HR and training press on how training groups can help their companies become high-performance organizations or high-performance work teams. In all of these articles, I have yet to see one that describes what the training function should do to adopt these high-performance principles and practices itself.

In the rush to new ISDL techniques, too much emphasis has been placed on the tools. Every week brings announcements of new tools to create CBT programs, Web-based training programs, knowledge-management repositories, and more. Unfortunately, many training organizations, rushing to meet their corporate mandates to move to ISDL, have become so enamored of these tools that they have forgotten the basic principles of good instructional design. I have seen many programs, both those developed within companies and those developed by independent producers for sale to companies, that use every new tool and special effect on the market, resulting in programs that look spectacular but have little value beyond entertainment.

Learn the new tools, but don't get so dazzled by their glitz that you forget about your roots in instructional design and learning theory. Use the new tools as appropriate, but remember that you don't always need all the bells and whistles of the latest-and-greatest tools to create excellent learning resources, and that many times the bells and whistles are more a distraction from learning than an aid to it.

Many traditional training organizations have balked at the mandate to move to ISDL because they believe that ISDL can never meet the high standards they have set for themselves for their traditional, instructor-led programs. I believe that the greatest service that the training group can provide to its company is to ensure that these same high-quality standards are applied to every method of instruction. The training group should review every potential acquisition for the company's ISDL library with the same high standards in mind. In my current role at Wang Global, I spend about 25 percent of my time reviewing programs from various suppliers, and I end up rejecting more than half of them because of quality issues.

The other new roles described in this chapter—teaching employees how to identify their personal learning needs and select appropriate learning methods, and coaching employees, managers, and knowledge resources—are vital to the success of ISDL. They will require new knowledge and skills on the part of the training staff, for example, coaching and consulting skills and the whole new field of knowledge management. These will be the topic of chapter 8.

LEARNING ASSIGNMENT

Review the last two large-scale training programs developed within your company. Consider the "Top 10 Questions to Ask When Choosing ISDL." Looking back and using these criteria, would you have taken a different approach to the development and delivery of these two programs? The "Top 10 Questions" are listed here to help you with this assignment.

1. Is any type of training or learning activity really going to solve the problem the company is facing?

2. Can the needed topics of instruction be defined for the vast majority of the target audience or will the success of the learning activity greatly depend on the ability of an instructor to adapt the content to audience needs in real time?

3. How much value comes from the personal interaction of the participants with an instructor or with other members of the class?

4. How much hands-on experience is required for the employee to master the learning content, that is, to take the information and turn it into personal knowledge?

5. What is the size of the target audience?

6. What is the cost of creating ISDL versus using traditional, instructor-led training methods?

7. How quickly does the training need to be done? How long will its value last before it has to be redone or before it is abandoned?

8. Is technology available to support learning activities? How accessible is that technology to your target audience?

9. Which resources are available to reinforce learning both as employees take an ISDL course and later as they apply their learning to their work?

10. How will the target audience respond to ISDL? What if you did no training of any type? How would people learn what they needed?

Chapter 7

Role of Technology-Based Training

S purred by continuous price reductions for personal computers, companies are moving rapidly to provide every employee with a PC or access to a PC, at least. Since organizations have invested so heavily in PCs and companywide networks, the pressure is on to use those PCs in every possible way, including as a means for training employees. Since the PCs themselves are a sunk cost, and since they are everywhere employees are, why not use them to train employees? That way, the company doesn't have to build classrooms, pay for travel to training sites, hire instructors, grant employees time away from the office for training, and the like. More and more companies are rushing to convert many, if not all, training programs to computer-based or Web-based training (CBT/WBT) as the primary means for ISDL.

Certainly, technology-based training plays an important role in most companies, but some technology zealots claim, "Computer-based training is ALWAYS better than classroom-based instruction." Instructor-led training programs, especially for some subjects, offer advantages that cannot be totally replaced by technology-based approaches to learning.

In this chapter, I will examine the major approaches to technology-based training that exist in today's marketplace along with their advantages and disadvantages. Before jumping into technology-based training, questions must be answered and some issues must be faced. These, too, will be discussed in this chapter.

TECHNOLOGY-BASED LEARNING

Every week, there are at least a few announcements of new technology-based learning solutions: new programs that you can buy intact, new tools for creating technology-based training programs, new services to deliver technology-based learning to your audiences, and so forth. New companies are being formed every month with great new ideas. As a corporate-training director, I get at least a dozen calls and letters each week from suppliers old and new. Professional magazines are filled with their glossy advertisements. Any national training conference will have 100 of more vendors displaying their latest wares. How do you make sense of it all? Let's start by defining some terms:

- synchronous versus asynchronous training
- computer-based training versus CD-ROM or multimedia programs versus Web-based training
- teleconferencing versus videoconferencing versus computer-conferencing
- training versus knowledge management versus performance technology/support
- distance learning
- individual versus group learning programs.

Synchronous versus Asynchronous

The term *synchronous* refers to a group of people taking an instructional program or watching a broadcast or holding a discussion at the same time. When you have a classroom-based program, all of the students are in the same room at the same time. Similarly, if you hold a video-, tele-, or computer-based conference, all of the participants are participating simultaneously.

In contrast, with *asynchronous* instruction, no two participants need to work at the same time. A computer-based training program that employees can access at any time is an example of an asynchronous program. Similarly, participating in a discussion forum, reading a book, and watching a videotape are asynchronous activities.

One of the advantages of technology-based learning is that it allows asynchronous learning—you don't have to bring many people together at the same time. Thus, it allows people to access learning resources when they need them and as they find time in their schedules. Asynchronous learning eliminates travel and dependence upon established training schedules.

One of the disadvantages of asynchronous learning is that it is generally more difficult for people being trained to discuss ideas with each other. Although discussion forums allow for some interaction among employees who are studying the same subject, they don't allow for the simultaneous discussions, such as that typical in a classroom forum. Often, people are reluctant to post a new idea on a discussion forum; in a classroom or meeting, a poor idea may be quickly forgotten, whereas a posting to a discussion forum tends to remain in full view for a long time.

Technology-based training can support synchronous learning, but its great strength is in supporting asynchronous learning. When considering whether to use technology-based training, you should always ask whether you want to do it synchronously or asynchronously. Table 7-1 lists some of the advantages and disadvantages of each mode.

CBT, CD-ROM, and WBT

Computer-based training refers to any type of training activity for which you use a computer. There are many forms of computer-based training, ranging from tutorials that are included in software packages to programs that you load from a floppy disk or CD-ROM to others that you download from a Web server within or outside your company.

Programs based upon CD-ROM technology generally are able to incorporate more live-action video and audio segments than other types of CBT. Because of the large storage capacity of a CD-ROM, the most visually splendid examples of CBT I have seen have been delivered via this medium.

Web-based training can range from simply downloading a simple CBT from the Web to live presentations. Because of network-bandwidth limitations (to be discussed later in this chapter), many video

Table 7-1. Synchronous versus asynchronous learning.

	ADVANTAGES	DISADVANTAGES
SYNCHRONOUS	—You know who is participating and when. —Discussions tend to be more open and richer. —Participants are able to ask questions and get clarifications immediately. —Participants can support and reinforce each other's learning.	—Participants need to convene at a fixed time, which may interrupt other important tasks. —Employees needing instruction must wait for the next scheduled session. —Discussion is often limited to the scheduled session. —Scheduling is difficult if participants are in different time zones.
ASYNCHRONOUS	—Employees participate according to their own needs and schedules. —Time zone differences are overcome.	—Ability to ask questions or get clarifications is limited while participating. —Employees may be shy about posting new or radical ideas on a discussion forum.

and audio segments that suppliers have tried to deliver via WBT have been relatively poor in quality or take so long to download from the Web that students become impatient and discouraged as they wait.

Recently, a number of online mentoring services have been introduced to the market to overcome one of the main problems of CBT: if you have a question or need a clarification while taking a CBT program, there is no one to ask. Among the suppliers of online mentoring and tutoring services for technical courses are Scholars.com, NetG, and DigitalThink.

Conferencing

Conferencing is a synchronous method of having people in different locations watch, listen to, or participate in the same event, be it a company announcement, a new product introduction, or a training program. The three common types of conference technology are teleconferencing, videoconferencing, and computer-based conferencing. Each has a unique set of advantages and disadvantages and differing cost structures.

Online Mentors at Wang Global

Most of Wang Global's employees who are working toward certification as MCSEs or MCSDs are using courseware that they download from our training Website or a local server or that is provided on CD-ROM. Many of these employees are also using an online mentoring service to answer their questions and receive feedback as they work through the CBT.

When students enroll with the online mentoring service for training, they can access the online mentors who are available to students 24 hours a day, seven days a week. If students have questions, they can enter a live discussion group at the service's Website or can send email to the mentors, who respond in six hours or less.

The student receives daily study questions via email from the online mentors. If the student answers the questions and returns the answers by email, the mentors review the answers and reply to indicate if the answers were right or wrong. This way, right answers are reinforced and explanations are given for incorrect responses.

Depending on the course being taken, the student may also receive online lab exercises and help-desk scenarios. As with the daily study questions, if the student sends in an assignment, it is reviewed and returned with comments.

When the student has completed a course and is preparing for a certification exam, the online mentoring service provides a practice exam to test the student's readiness.

Online mentoring services help fill the gap left by CBT—someone is there to answer questions and give feedback. Many of the Wang Global employees who are using this service say that it is an invaluable service for them.

Teleconferencing is the oldest method and relies upon telephones. Either using company-owned capabilities or working through a teleconferencing provider, many people can participate in the same telephone conversation. Teleconferences with many participants usually are limited to a presentation; if you have several dozen people on the line, it is difficult to establish a multi-way dialogue. Often, in large teleconferences, questions will be taken by fax or email. Teleconferences are relatively easy to set up and cost little more than the phone charges to call in.

Teleconferencing can be combined with other methods to improve the quality of instruction. For example, it is often advisable to provide (by mail, fax, or email) participants with a set of slides or other materials that they can follow as they listen to the speaker.

Videoconferencing is the most expensive of the three methods, often requiring satellite dishes at both the sending and receiving locations. Some larger companies have set up their own video networks for videoconferencing. Newer technologies allow transmission over telephone lines, but you need multiple high-speed lines to enable full-motion video. With lesser transmission capability, the picture quality suffers and the motions of the participants seem unsteady. Some hotel chains and at least one office-services company also have videoconferencing capabilities that they will rent out to companies. Transmission to multiple sites is usually done in only one direction, that is, people can watch the speaker, but the speaker cannot see the people. Questions can be asked via telephone, fax, or email.

Some education providers regularly use videoconferencing. For example, National Technological University (NTU) is a consortium of universities and companies, which provides a wide array of mostly technical courses to its members over a satellite broadcast network. Members pay an annual membership fee plus a fee for each program they sign up to receive. Programs are broadcast live with questions coming back by phone. Members also have the option of recording broadcasts for viewing at other times.

Computer-based conferencing has greatly improved over the past several years with the introduction of several very good products. At its best, computer-based conferencing gives each participant a screen divided into several frames. In one frame is a "talking head" of the speaker with live audio and video. A second frame contains the speaker's slides and exhibits. A third frame enables live questions to come from the audience or allows the audience to vote on questions posed by the speaker.

These conferences can be accessed by anyone on the network or can be limited to specific users. They can be arranged in minutes (with the proper tools and IS support). They can also handle multiple speakers in multiple locations with relatively inexpensive equipment.

Giving a Seminar for NTU

In 1994, NTU invited me to give a five-hour seminar from one of its member schools, Arizona State University. I received very precise instructions for the format and for the preparation of materials to use in the seminar.

The sponsor asked me if I would prefer them to invite local people to attend the seminar (along with the audiences at the other end of the satellite links). This seemed like a good idea—I didn't relish the idea of spending five hours talking to a camera in an empty room.

About a dozen companies and university sites had signed up for the seminar, but I didn't receive a single question via the telephone line. In retrospect, I should have created some strategies for audience involvement. The sponsor told me that it was not unusual to have no one at the other end of the broadcasts, because, most times, there is a videocassette recorder at the other end, and people watch the videotapes at their leisure. In reality, this synchronous training activity was transformed into an asynchronous activity.

Talking to an empty room can be disconcerting for speakers/trainers. The strategies for doing effective videoconferences and long-distance training via a video network are very different from those used for typical classroom presentations. For example, with only a camera operator in the room, you cannot rely on students' body language to gauge how your presentation is being received. And although you can ask students at remote sites to call in questions, there is little or no opportunity for a true class discussion. Speakers need to be prepared for this different type of assignment.

Finally, once the company has invested in the conferencing software, there is little or no marginal cost for each new conference.

The disadvantage of this type of conference has to do mainly with the quality of the audio and video reception. Depending on the bandwidth available on the network, the video portion can range from near-television quality to a very unstable picture. Because the video is in such a small frame on the screen, some people find it difficult to watch, even if the transmission quality is good, and decide to turn off the video and just listen to the audio portion.

Knowledge Management and Performance Technology/Support

Knowledge management refers to a company's efforts to keep track of its knowledge assets, categorize and store those assets, and make them available to be used throughout the company. Knowledge management and how to build a corporate-knowledge network are the subjects of the next chapter. Knowledge management is not a traditional area of specialization or expertise for the training organization. Training groups should lead the way in knowledge management, because a good knowledge-management system can quickly become what trainers now call human performance improvement (HPI) or performance support.

Human performance improvement, according to Jim Fuller (1999), "is a systemic and systematic approach to identifying the barriers that prevent people from achieving top performance that contributes to the success of the organization. We then create solutions that quickly and effectively remove the barriers so people can improve their performance and achieve their full potential."

The job of HRD professionals goes beyond merely removing barriers, however. It extends to *performance support*—making help available to people as they do their jobs. For example, as I use Microsoft Word to write this chapter, if I have a question on how to use a particular feature, I can click on the question-mark icon. Up pops a winking, paperclip-cartoon character along with a text box that asks me, "What would you like to do?" I can then type in a question and get immediate help on that particular feature of the product. Similarly, in many call-center operations, customer service representatives have a database of common questions and answers that they can query if they do not know the answer to a particular caller's question.

Some years ago, on a visit to Caterpillar, company representatives showed me a set of plastic models of common welding errors that had been made by some of their smaller subcontractors. If there was a problem with the quality of the subcontractor's welding, they could call the subcontractor, and, rather than trying to describe the problem over the telephone, they could say, "Look at model #17—that's what your weld looks like."

Such performance support tools cannot be called "training" in the traditional sense, but they are learning aids. And they are the best type of learning aids, those known as just-in-time and just-enough. They are available at the precise moment the employee has a learning need, and they are just sufficient to solve the immediate problem.

One of the challenges to the traditional training community is to stop thinking in terms of "programs" and start thinking in terms of "chunks"—learning segments of short duration that focus on a single topic or skill.

Training Chunks Versus Training Programs

In the mid-1980s, when I was in charge of network training at Digital Equipment Corporation, I proposed a new method for training networks-sales and sales-support people through a program that was eventually called Network University. The model brought together 500 or so field personnel for a week. During that week, we ran 40 to 70 different sessions, ranging from one hour to three full days depending on the complexity of the topic.

When I first proposed this model to Digital's educational services group, I was told, "This isn't the way we do training." For 20 years, Digital's training had been composed of one-week, lecture-lab courses, each on a single product. For example, the course on Digital's networking software ran for five days and covered everything: how to sell the product, how to install and test it, how to fix it, how to write device drivers for it, and more. To the traditional training group at Digital, this was a training program.

I didn't consider the Network University program to be a *training* program; I thought of it as a *learning* program. It provided what people needed to learn so that they could get their jobs done. The employees themselves (with some input from corporate groups) primarily determined the topics for each program. The program was very popular, because employees knew that we would respond to their stated learning needs instead of pushing out reams of material designed by corporate people who didn't live in the world of the field employee.

(continued on next page)

Training Chunks Versus Training Programs
(continued)

The length of each session at Network University was determined by how much material needed to be covered. If it required an hour, it got an hour. If it needed two or three days, that's what it got. I had never heard of the term *chunking* at that time, but that's what we did.

Chunking is one of those great ideas that make a lot of sense, but somehow trainers have gotten stuck in the paradigm about how long a proper training program should be. Whether a day or a week, most traditional training programs have focused on relatively long segments of instruction. Perhaps it came from the notion that you want to get people away from their jobs and thinking about training. Of course, that's easier when they devote an entire day or an entire week to training. Perhaps trainers thought, "We're bringing all of these people into the training center, and since they're making the trip, we might as well keep them here a whole week and see what we can give them that will be useful."

Perhaps it was because it made it easier to schedule training facilities and trainers' schedules when you think in terms of days or weeks. Many times I have spent several days in a training program, only to think later, "You know, there was about four hours of really good material in that program that I needed, but the rest of the time was a waste."

If you consider the four-stage learning model (figure 1-1), chunking makes even more sense. When you chunk material and make it easy to find and use, you help employees find the information they need to improve their job performance. By giving them the chunk that they need right at this moment, they can immediately apply it to their work, thereby turning that information into knowledge. Have you ever been faced by a situation at work and thought, "There was something in that training program I took a few months back that applied to this situation, but I can't remember what it was"? In this situation, you either have to solve the problem *de novo,* or you have to spend hours locating the old training materials and hunting through them to find the answer. Sometimes you find it, and sometimes you don't (especially if the organization of your office is as random as mine!).

The other admirable characteristic of performance support is that people seek out exactly what they need. Employees determine their own learning needs and then pinpoint the learning resources within the performance-support system to help them learn. This is true ISDL. It represents a change in orientation from training, wherein a trainer or instructional designer determines the content of training, to real learning, wherein the learner identifies the learning need.

Distance Learning

The U.S. Distance Learning Association (1999) defines distance learning as "the acquisition of knowledge and skills through mediated information and instruction, encompassing all technologies and other forms of learning at a distance." That is a very broad definition. Basically, distance learning spans the gamut of technologies: satellite broadcasts, video-, tele-, and computer-based conferencing, and asynchronous delivery of information for the purpose of learning. Here, I will discuss just a few relevant examples, namely NTU, the Business Channel, and Learn2.com.

National Technological University. An alliance of companies and universities, NTU (1999) is a leading provider of advanced technical education and training using distance-learning technologies via a satellite network. Its goal is to deliver college-level technical courses directly to the worksite to eliminate travel costs and time away from the job. Its customers range from IBM to Hewlett-Packard to Motorola to the U.S. Departments of Defense and Energy. What distinguishes NTU from many distance-learning programs is that it is a true, accredited, degree-granting university, although NTU also provides a wide range of noncredit courses.

The Business Channel. The Business Channel (1999) delivers both technical and management training to its customers via satellite broadcasts and online instruction. For example, working in partnership with the Massachusetts Institute of Technology, it recently offered a six-week course on Internet commerce. Each week, an MIT professor delivered a live seminar broadcast. During the broadcast, participants could submit questions via telephone, fax, or email. There were reading assignments and online discussions moderated by the professor or other MIT teaching assistants. This same course will soon be delivered online. The video segments will be chunked and delivered through streaming video technology. The Business Channel was bought from the Public Broadcasting System several months ago by NTU and is now a division of NTU.

check it out ✗

Learn2.com. An example of true, just-in-time learning, Learn2.com (1999) is a fascinating free Website that includes lessons on many practical skills: how to shop for a wireless telephone, how to perform a breast self-examination, how to fry an egg, and more. For example, just before Mother's Day, it featured a lesson on how to gift wrap a present. It is a very good example of the possibilities of using a Website to provide chunks of training and learning without a formal instructor.

Distance Learning for Project Management at Wang Global

At Wang Global, we recently undertook our first distance-learning program. In designing a companywide, project-management curriculum, we used a combination of self-paced training (a book, a CD-ROM-based instructional program, and a CBT program), an instructor-led seminar, and a series of distance-learning courses.

The distance-learning courses, provided by the International School of Information Management (1999) are academic-type courses requiring outside reading, written assignments, and class discussion, but the delivery is done over the Internet through ISIM's Website. The courses require between eight and 14 hours of work per week for each student. While ISIM offers college credit for these courses, Wang Global's primary purpose for the courses is to prepare employees to become certified as project-management professionals (PMPs) by the Project Management Institute.

The project-management training strategy allows employees to gain the project-management skills needed by the company to run its business and to achieve professional certification while spending only one week in a live seminar away from the office. Other university programs on project management that we investigated included up to 12 weeks of live seminars to achieve the same goals.

The other very useful feature of the ISIM distance-learning courses is that they can provide the distance-learning discussions and interactions with the instructor in a variety of languages. For example, Wang Global is running one ISIM course series for employees from Mexico, Venezuela, Chile, and Colombia. For these sessions, ISIM has arranged to have a Spanish-speaking instructor available, although the textbooks are in English.

By using distance learning for these courses, we are able to eliminate the costs of travel and time away from the office for employees who are studying for the PMI certification exam. We are also able to accommodate differing schedules and multiple time zones; each class has employees from many different countries. At the time of this writing, the course is still ongoing, but employees have reported good experiences with it.

Hundreds of distance-learning providers operate in dozens of countries on today's market, ranging from traditional colleges and universities to virtual universities that exist only in online form, from nonprofit professional organizations to for-profit distance-learning companies, from public school systems to free, Internet-based resources.

Distance learning is growing rapidly and should be considered as an important component of any ISDL strategy. Early distance-learning efforts, such as NTU, relied on satellite broadcasts, requiring large investments in transmission and reception equipment, as well as the substantial costs for satellite time. With the advent of streaming technologies for Web broadcasts, both Internet and intranet, little investment is needed beyond what many companies are already spending on their internal networks. Web-based distance learning also affords the opportunity for employees to learn at home, as long as they have a PC and access to an Internet service provider.

Individual Versus Group Learning Programs

When the topic of ISDL comes up for discussion, the first assumption that many people make is that all work is done by the individual, with no group classes, group interaction, group learning, or group reinforcement. This assumption is both true and false. It is true in that the individual chooses the time and place to learn and is not generally dependent on the schedules of other people studying the same subject (except with the synchronous methods of conferencing). Books, tapes, CBTs, and Web-based training are available 24 hours a day, seven days a week, with no time off for holidays or vacations. So if the individual employee prefers to learn alone, ISDL is a perfect solution.

On the other hand, the assumption that all work is done on an individual basis is often false, because participating in ISDL does not mandate that you study alone. There are many positive aspects to group study, among them are the following:

- Through discussion and dialogue with other students, you may improve your own understanding.
- Other students in a class may ask questions that are valuable to you, but which you may not have raised yourself.
- Other students in your group can help reinforce your learning as you later try to apply your learning to your work (assuming that no instructor or manager is available to help).
- By working in a group, you get to know others who can share their knowledge with you, helping you to build your personal network, inside or outside the company, that can lead to friendships, job opportunities, and so forth in the future.

The key here is to create a PLE in your company so that people are ready, willing, and able to share their knowledge and skills with others. The many capabilities and tools of the company's knowledge network can make this possible.

BARRIERS TO TECHNOLOGY-BASED TRAINING

Even if your company has PCs everywhere and an extensive corporate network, barriers remain to using technology-based learning. At Wang Global, we have several thousand employees studying for Microsoft certifications using computer-based training as the primary learning method. The courseware was installed on our corporate intranet, accessible through our training Website. Even though Wang Global is a "networked technology services and solutions" company, there were

Group Learning at Wang Global

In the project-management curriculum at Wang Global, we are relying heavily on group learning. Although the introductory materials are self-paced and are sent to each individual, the weeklong seminar brings together a group of people who not only attend the class together, but work through a case study in small groups throughout the week.

When these employees return to their respective offices, they can use a discussion forum on our intranet to continue discussions, ask questions of each other, share experiences as they implement what they have learned, point to other resources they have found that they think will be of interest or value to others, and so forth. When many of these employees then sign up for the ISIM distance-learning courses, they are working both individually and in groups. Individually, they do their reading and assignments, but the ISIM virtual classroom includes class discussions, with the instructor and with each other, on the ISIM Website. These discussions are asynchronous; students post their comments when they have time to get on the site and leave those comments there for others to read and respond to at their convenience. Someone may ask a question and find answers coming back over the next several days.

Generally, whether in a real or a virtual classroom, students report that much of the value of the learning experience comes from group interaction. Even though the ISIM distance-learning classes can be classified as ISDL, they spark a great deal of group interaction.

---

many barriers—human, desktop, and network—to worldwide implementation. These barriers will be the topics of the next few sections.

Human Barriers

Some people just don't like using CBT. They spend their workdays staring at a computer screen, and they don't want to have to use the same computer to study. For other, more experienced employees who already know much of the subject matter, CBT is too slow: "You can only hit the enter button so fast." They prefer to use books so they can skim over the chapters they know and focus on those that are new or different.

At Wang Global, we also had some problems with language barriers. Although English is the standard tongue of the computer industry, and most Wang Global employees can read English quite well, the fact that our suppliers' courseware was provided exclusively in English created some real barriers. An even greater problem was the online mentoring service, which worked only in English. For many people, English was a second language, so reading was easier than conversing or writing. Some employees, who knew enough English to take the CBT courses, did not write English well enough to feel at ease communicating with their online mentors. In several countries, we provided employees with other types of self-study materials in their local language. In still other countries, local management decided to use local training providers who would do the training in the local language. Even though these alternative strategies added to the company's training budget, they were based on sound judgments by local country management.

By far, the greatest human barrier to ISDL is time. Many employees already work 10 or 20 hours of overtime per week. Add to that family and personal responsibilities, and they can't find any other time in their schedules for training.

When a company moves to ISDL, it has to pay attention to time issues. When a manager sends someone to a class, that person will be absent from the office for a period of time. When that same employee decides to take an ISDL program, the manager still expects him or her to be in the office working. As with most learning activities, on the job or in college, the best strategy is to set aside specific times for learning. I have seen some employees post signs on their office doors: "In training until 4:00 p.m.—DO NOT DISTURB."

When an employee is sent to a training program for a week or more, the company often recognizes the employee in some way—a certificate, some recognition on his or her personnel record, and so forth. Often, being sent to corporate headquarters to attend a program is itself a reward; the employee has some time off from work plus travel and expenses. Nevertheless, few companies have found any way of providing similar recognition for employees taking ISDL. This is a need that companies need to address to foster ISDL throughout their organizations.

Desktop Barriers

As companies have built up their stocks of personal computers, they have purchased many different models with different features, speeds, and accessories. This can create a number of barriers to the implementation of CBT, such as the following:

- If many of your company's PCs do not have CD-ROM drives, you will have to consider the cost of adding those drives if you want to use CD-ROM-based instructional programs.
- Many CBT programs, designed to be down-loaded from a server to the student's PC, require large amounts of disk space. If your company's PCs don't have enough disk space, the same programs may sometimes be used in live-play mode from the server, but there is often a noticeable difference in performance, sometimes so noticeable that it discourages the learner.
- If you plan to use PCs to play instructional programs that have audio or video components, or if you plan to use them as part of a computer-based-conferencing system, you need to make certain that they have both audio and video capabilities, as well as the correct utility software.
- In some situations, many employees share a few PCs, so there may not be a sufficient number of PCs to cover the learning needs of employees and support other ongoing work.
- To study effectively, employees need an environment that is relatively quiet and free from distractions. In many workplace settings, neither of these requirements is met, making the workplace an undesirable setting for learning.

One last consideration is that these problems can become exacerbated if you ask employees to use their own PCs at home to take the training on their own time. For many people, home PCs are a luxury for which they have not budgeted, and for many others, their home PCs are even more outdated than the ones they use at the office.

Network Barriers

At Wang Global, our intention was to make all of our CBT courses available over the corporate network, allowing employees to either download the courses to their local PCs or to play them in live mode directly from the corporate server. We had to modify this strategy almost immediately because we encountered a number of issues.

Because Wang Global had grown rapidly over the previous several years by acquiring other companies, with locations scattered across more than 40 countries, not all parts of the company were immediately part of the company's global network. And since the server on which the courseware resided was within the company's intranet, not every employee in every country had access to it. We had to set up a number of local courseware servers to provide local access to the CBT courseware. We solved some of this problem with the help of the online mentoring service, which allowed our employees to download the CBT courseware from their Internet-based servers. In the near future, we will move our server beyond Wang Global's firewall so that employees will be able to access the courseware both using the company's intranet and over the Internet (with the appropriate security precautions).

Even where a country's local network was integrated into the company's global network, in some countries the national telecommunications infrastructure was relatively weak and slow. The CBT-courseware files tend to be large, and, therefore, require a relatively long time to download, placing a burden on a company's telecommunications infrastructure that was not designed to handle these large downloads regularly. The solution to this problem was to install the courseware on local company servers in some countries.

A substantial portion of Wang Global's business involves placing employees within secure government facilities or within corporate customers' IS organizations. In many cases, government or corporate IS firewalls made it impossible for employees to reach the Wang Global network. In these situations, we had to provide employees with the courseware on CD-ROMs so that they could run them on their local PCs.

The lesson to draw from Wang Global's experience is this: Before moving to a network-based or Web-based training solution, you need to closely examine the capabilities of your network and whether your target audience will indeed be able to access that solution.

THE ROLE OF TECHNOLOGY-BASED LEARNING

Technology-based learning has a lot to offer any company. Every day, more tools and techniques are introduced to make technology-based learning easier to develop, easier to use, more effective in delivering learning resources to the individual—all at lower and lower costs. No technology is a panacea for any company's learning needs. Remember that technology-based learning still represents only a small portion of most companies' investments in employee training. According to research analyst Judy Lamont (1999), "Electronic training techniques still account for only 20 percent of instructional time, but that is double the percent of a year ago and headed up to 50 percent within the next couple of years."

Technology-based learning must be of high quality. When people go to an instructor-led course, they will generally stay in the class for the duration, even if the instructor gets off to a rocky start or if the first part of the course doesn't seem relevant to their work. In such situations, students often use each other for support or take maximum opportunity to learn from each other if the instructor is not providing what they need. In the world of technology-based learning, however, students generally don't exhibit the same patience.

KEEPING UP WITH INNOVATIONS

With all of the advances of technology-based learning and with the many excellent products and services available on today's market, every company should examine the role that technology-based learning can and should play in its overall training/learning strategy. At the same time, companies should not rush headlong into technology-based learning without examining whether it will solve the problems they face.

Keeping up with all of the new products and services can itself be a daunting challenge. Attending the Interactive Multimedia conference and TechKnowledge conferences sponsored by the American Society for Training & Development, the Masie Center's annual

TechLearn conference, or Lakewood Publications' annual On-Line Learning Conference can certainly give you a quick education on what the technology-based-learning field has to offer. You can also subscribe to free email newsletters from those organizations to help keep up with the latest news and trends.

LEARNING ASSIGNMENT

Inventory the methods of technology-based training being used in your company (not just those being used by the training group itself). Do employees have the necessary tools and technologies to utilize technology-based training? If not, meet with the company's IS organization to discuss what needs to be done to enable every employee to use technology-based training. Hint: One way of sparking the interest of the IS group in TBT is to start with their own learning needs.

When you examine the technology-based training being done in your organization, consider the following questions:

- Why did you choose this particular technology?
- Who is the target audience for the training?
- Do all members of the target audience have the appropriate technology available to use the training?
- What alternatives are available for delivering this training?
- What are the advantages and disadvantages of the selected learning method?
- How effectively is the selected learning method helping individuals, the group, and the company meet their business goals?
- How can you improve the learning experience, the retention of learning, and the application of learning to the job by using a combination of learning methods?

Chapter 8

Building and Using a Knowledge Network

Britton Manasco (1999) says that the two primary approaches to knowledge management are managing content and managing connections. The idea of a knowledge network (Tobin 1997) encompasses both of these approaches and adds two more major elements: providing individual learning resources and pointers to learning resources on the network, and furnishing individual and group-learning tools as part of the network. I'll start this chapter with an explanation of these four major elements of a knowledge network and then describe the role of a knowledge network in ISDL. I will also address how the corporate-training group can build and use the knowledge network to help the company and its employees meet their collective and individual learning goals.

A knowledge network is an integrated set of tools and databases that enable the company and its employees to gather, store, find, and learn from information that can help to improve individual and corporate results over time. The four major elements of a knowledge network are shown in table 8-1.

Table 8-1. Elements of a knowledge network.

KNOWLEDGE-NETWORK ELEMENT	CONTENTS
Content database	Explicit knowledge derived from individual employees, teams, and other internal and external sources
Connections database	Pointers to individual employees and teams throughout the company and sometimes its customers and suppliers, who are sources of tacit knowledge
Learning-resources database	Pointers to internal and external learning resources (courses, libraries, employee performance support systems, seminars, symposia, and so forth) and access to those learning resources available through the network
Individual and group-learning facilitators	Tools that enable discussion and dialogue between learners (those seeking knowledge) and learning resources

Companies have created huge databases to store technical specifications, customer information, research data, market information, and much more. These databases were designed so employees can learn from each other's experiences, avoid repeating others' errors, and avoid reinventing the wheel.

What goes into the content database is explicit knowledge—knowledge that is easy to represent in the words, tables, charts, and diagrams that can be coded into an electronic format. Tacit knowledge, that which is not easily expressed in electronic form, cannot be placed into the storehouse. Tacit knowledge resides in the minds of individual employees and can be accessed only through discussion and dialogue. In the field of artificial intelligence, attempts have been made over the past 20 years to develop "expert systems" to capture tacit knowledge. To develop an expert system, a researcher works with the expert over time to understand his or her thinking process and then develops a rule-based program to simulate the expert's thinking process.

In chapter 6, I told the story of a company's attempt to develop an expert system to simulate the thinking process of its expert on

Reinventing the Wheel

"Have you ever spent hours, days, or even weeks solving a problem at work, only to discover later that someone else in the company had already solved that problem and perhaps had developed a better solution than you did?" I often start presentations on knowledge management with this question, and usually every person in the audience can recall this type of experience.

If you don't know that a solution to your problem exists, for all practical purposes it doesn't exist. If you don't know that Joe in the next cubicle or Diana over in the company's Singapore office faced this same problem and solved it last week or last year, it is a new problem and requires a new solution. One of the primary purposes of a knowledge network is to enable you to find out if the problem has been encountered previously and, if so, how it was solved.

Construction-industry giant Bechtel Corporation (Marshall, Prusak & Shpilberg 1996) requires every project team to write a report on the problems encountered and the solutions developed and to put that report into a database. When a new project team is assembled to start a new project, it is required to review the reports on all similar projects so that they can learn from others' experiences, even before they start to plan the new project. Bechtel's knowledge-management system focuses on managing content but also helps with managing connections. If a team is facing a problem not seen in the reports, they can check the reports for the names of employees who worked on similar projects and contact them to discuss the new problem—a way of uncovering those employees' tacit knowledge.

---

reading seismic graphs. The result was a good expert system that reached the 80–85 percent level in emulating the real expert. At the same time, the person who developed the system learned even more through the process of discussion, dialogue, and demonstration than he could translate into the rules for the computer program. That extra 15–20 percent was tacit knowledge that couldn't be made explicit. This is why some knowledge-management systems focus on connecting people who need to develop new knowledge and those who already have it.

To uncover a person's tacit knowledge requires first that you know that that person exists. In today's multinational companies, it is unlikely that any one employee will know everyone else or even know of most people who work for the company outside the individual's local operation. This is why some knowledge-management systems focus on making connections between people.

The connections database provides information on individual employees and teams throughout the company and sometimes includes information on customers and suppliers, as well as external consultants and contractors and their areas of expertise and experience. The connections database can be searched by employees who are seeking a knowledge or learning resource. Employees can use this database to identify potential team members for a new project, find the solution to a problem they are facing, locate a coach as they learn a new skill or try to master a new knowledge area, or gather intelligence for a proposal.

The learning-resources database is a source for finding the courses, materials, or people that employees need to meet personal learning needs. Learning resources come from many places:

- the traditional training group's catalog and schedule of courses
- online courses available over the network
- an employee performance support system
- the corporate library or an external library accessible through the network, including live links to Websites inside and outside the company
- the content database
- the connections database, where the learning resource is a person rather than a course or published learning materials.

If the company's training group has developed learning guides, as discussed in chapter 6, those guides would be an integral part of this section of the knowledge network, guiding employees to any and all of the learning resources listed previously.

Individual and group-learning facilitators are tools that enable the employee to use the first three elements of the knowledge network. They include tools to

- search the content and connections databases

- take courses available from the learning-resources database
- contact individuals listed in the connections database and to conduct discussions and dialogues
- identify others who are interested in studying the same subject, who can then help reinforce learning activities.

John Seely Brown, of Xerox Corporation's Palo Alto Research Center, tells of research on how field-service technicians actually learn how to repair Xerox equipment. Their research showed that formal training programs were not the primary means of learning, but that technicians learned most effectively by experimenting and then sharing ideas and experiences and stories with each other around the water cooler or in the lunchroom. As Brown states, "In a sense, these stories are the real 'expert systems' used by tech-reps on the job. They are a storehouse of past problems and diagnoses, a template for constructing a theory about the current problem, and the basis for making an educated stab at a solution" (Brown 1998).

The knowledge network provides tools for carrying out these dialogues among technicians who don't have real opportunities to meet over the water cooler or in the lunchroom. It also provides a mechanism for storing the information in organizational memory, the content database of a knowledge network. Speculating on the best way to share these types of both explicit and tacit knowledge, Brown goes on to say, "One possibility is to create advanced multimedia information systems that would make it easier for reps and other employees to plug in to this collective social mind. Such a system might allow the reps to pass around annotated video clips of useful stories . . . By commenting on each other's experiences, reps could refine and disseminate new knowledge."

Many tools are available in today's market for building a knowledge network. No single tool will do the complete job for any company, and since new tools are being introduced into the market at an astounding rate, you should examine the full spectrum of available products before starting out. In the next section, I will discuss some important considerations in building a knowledge network to enhance its usefulness to employees and to the company. After all, a knowledge network is only valuable if it is actually used by employees in their work and if it enables and supports ISDL.

IMPORTANT CONSIDERATIONS FOR A KNOWLEDGE NETWORK

No matter how much time, effort, and expense you invest in building your company's knowledge network, you will get no return on that investment unless employees find it both useful and usable. The next few sections cover some important considerations to keep in mind for each of the four major components of the knowledge network.

The Content Database

Too many companies start out by converting all of their documentation into HTML or some database format and then say that they have created a knowledge-management system. Nothing could be further from the truth. Before starting to build the content database, you need to consider what information employees need and how it can best be organized and accessed. The following ideas can help you organize your knowledge-management system:

- *Make it current.* If the content database contains old information, employees won't find it useful. If they don't find it useful, they won't use it. You need to plan not just for the initial implementation of the database, but also for its constant refreshing by adding new content and purging outdated information.

- *Make it accurate.* If you use information extracted from the database, and you find that the information was wrong, caused you embarrassment, or caused you to make an incorrect decision, you'll never trust it again. You need experts to review material before it is entered into the database to ensure its accuracy and its alignment with company policies and the organization's strategic business directions.

- *Make it dynamic.* Anyone in the organization should be able to suggest content. Of course, all content should be checked for accuracy before entering it into the database. For example, if an employee attends a professional conference and collects papers and presentations from that conference, those materials rarely travel out of the person's office or are circulated through his or her work group. That employee should consider putting valuable, useful materials from presentations into the content database for use by others in the company.

- *Make it easy to use.* People don't want to have to hunt through more than a few screens of content to find what they need. Recently, I used one library system to search for articles on the topic of electronic commerce. This search system returned 3,600 articles without a way of further indexing them—not a very user-friendly system. A number of more sophisticated search tools are available on the market for these purposes. Organize it logically. Take the time and effort to index the content by keywords so that it is easy for people to find what they need.

Sharing Information From a Conference

Several years ago, I participated in a conference of training professionals. Just before my own presentation, there was a general session featuring an outstanding speaker, whose messages had relevance not only to the audience of trainers, but also to the general management of the companies represented by the trainers.

In my session, I talked about creating a knowledge network to share knowledge and ideas throughout a company. At one point, I asked how many people had attended the general session. All of the 100 people in the room raised their hands. I asked, "How many of you believed that the speaker's ideas had value for others in your company from the CEO on down?" All 100 hands again went up.

"How many of you plan to buy the tape of the speaker's session or a copy of his book and give it to your CEO or to others in your company?" Only three hands went up and all the hands belonged to trainers—the people whose job it is to spread new knowledge in their companies!

Think of the value that could be brought to the company if people attending conferences would carry back ideas and share them through the knowledge network. You might not know who in the company could benefit from a speaker's ideas, but through the knowledge network you can at least put the ideas out there for consideration by anyone who might be interested.

- *Give credit where credit is due.* Acknowledge those who contribute material for the database. Along with providing a psychic reward to contributors, this will facilitate making people connections within the company.

- *Reward people for contributing to the database.* Contributions can be both positive and negative—positive in adding or suggesting new content and negative in correcting errors and reporting failed efforts.

- *Examine other ways for using the content.* By tracking the usage of various segments of the content database, you may discover other uses for it. For example, if one section is accessed many times, it may point out a common learning need or frequently encountered problem. That, in turn, may suggest the need for revising a basic training program or the need to make changes to one of the company's products.

The Connections Database

Some companies have begun work on a connections database by starting with a résumé database. Some have invested in developing a sophisticated competencies database. Although both of these are good starts, they are not sufficient to meet the basic purpose of the knowledge network—to enable employees to find others in the company who have knowledge and skills that would benefit their work. For each person included, the connections database should contain information on educational background, work background, skills and competencies, and other relevant information.

For educational background, include not only colleges attended and degrees granted, but major and minor courses of study, and other special degrees or certificates. For example, reporting a degree in computer science isn't enough to know what skills an employee may have. You need to know which programming languages, which database systems, and so forth that the employee knows. Similarly, merely listing a master's degree in business administration doesn't tell you whether the person has studied marketing, finance, accounting, or information systems. It may also be useful in today's global economy to know what languages the employee reads, speaks, or writes and the level of proficiency in each of those skills. Furthermore, employees

Reporting Negative Results

The story goes like this: An archeology professor was sentenced to prison for violating a local law in a remote country where he was doing research. He was put into a cell with another archeology professor—a man who had some renown in the field but who had been reported missing some 10 years earlier. The prison conditions were deplorable.

After a few weeks, the new prisoner devised an escape plan. He reviewed it with his cellmate and offered to take him along. The old professor wished his colleague good luck but declined to accompany him. That night, the new prisoner made his escape.

Three days later, the escapee was captured and returned to the cell. "You can't imagine the difficulties I had in the desert. The heat! The insects! My water ran out and what I found was undrinkable!"

"I know," said his cellmate. "Shortly after I was imprisoned here, I tried to escape, and my plan was almost identical to yours. I was back here in three days also."

"What!" the man screamed. "Why didn't you tell me?"

"Who publishes negative results?" replied the old professor with a shrug.

Although it rarely happens in academia, there can be great value in publishing negative results on your company's knowledge network. If an employee has followed a logical course of action and ended up with negative results, he or she can potentially save many others from following that same logic, thereby leading to additional negative results. If the employee warns others through the knowledge network, they can avoid a seemingly reasonable approach that will inevitably lead to failure. An old proverb goes, "It is a wise man who learns from the mistakes of others," but that cannot happen if you never learn of the errors that others have made.

---

may have other special skills that aren't obvious from a list of educational credentials—subjects that they may have studied on their own or through continuing education courses or company-sponsored training programs.

A résumé database typically covers the time before an employee started working for your company. It lists employers and job titles, perhaps with a few bullets about major accomplishments in each job. The connections database requires more detail, such as skills used and mastered in each job assignment, industry knowledge developed, customers served, and so forth, not only for previous employers, but also in the person's career within your own company. You might also want to list special assignments the person has undertaken, such as leading a new product introduction task force, rotational assignments, or heading up the company's United Way campaign.

A person's complete set of skills and competencies will typically not be fully represented by a sketch of his or her educational background or work history. Create a complete listing for each employee in the connections database. It is often surprising to find out that fellow workers have a wide array of skills that you never would have guessed. Perhaps they worked in family businesses unrelated to their current careers, or maybe they have long-held avocational interests.

The connections database should also contain any other relevant or potentially relevant information about the employee, such as professional memberships, magazine and journal subscriptions, presentations made at conferences, and so on.

Keep the connections database current and accurate. Employees continually add to their backgrounds by taking courses, joining new professional organizations, taking on new assignments, and a host of other means. The best way of ensuring that the database remains current is to give employees the responsibility for maintaining their own records. At first, there should be a common format imposed, so that information is consistently classified and more easily collected for the initial implementation of the database, but employees should update their profiles at least annually and, preferably, whenever there is new information to add.

The Learning-Resources Database

The learning-resources database should be very broad in content. While the content database may be limited to official company documents, there should be no such restrictions on the learning resource database. If an employee reads an article or gets a presentation or paper from a conference he or she has attended, the employee should be able to post it in the learning-resources database. Of course, employees must pay attention to copyright restrictions, but at the least, they can summarize the document in the database and provide instructions on how to obtain a copy.

You should also allow employees to add information they receive through other learning resources, such as local conferences, the offerings of local colleges and universities, local chapters of professional organizations, and the like. It is virtually impossible for any central organization, whether a training group, the IS organization, or a specialized knowledge-management group, to keep track of all of the learning resources available to employees scattered throughout the world and working in many different professions. Rather than asking employees to send notices to a central group (which would be flooded by the volume of mail), it is much easier and faster to allow employees to add listings on their own.

A more controversial recommendation is to let employees add editorial comments to any of these listings, such as:

- "I took the 'Statistics for Business' course at University X, while a colleague took a similar course at Y College. After comparing our notes and experiences, we would both recommend the course at Y College."

- "I went to the National Conference of this professional organization twice in the past three years. It has never been well organized, and it is mainly a platform for suppliers to show their latest wares. If you are interested in seeing the latest products, it is worth the trip, but don't expect to get much out of the educational sessions."

Although you have to careful with these types of comments so as not to libel anyone, they can add a lot of value and keep people from wasting their time and the company's money by going to poor programs.

Individual and Group-Learning Facilitators

Sometimes referred to as groupware, individual and group learning facilitators are the tools that enable employees to use the knowledge network. Tools also help employees learn individually and as groups from the resources within and identified by the knowledge network and the people resources they have found in the connections database. The company's IS department should include a set of these tools in the standard user configuration. Although there are many different tools on the market, the IS group should work with the training group and end users to select an appropriate set. The tools should include capabilities starting with email and continuing through streaming audio and video technologies, CD-ROM capabilities, courseware servers, electronic-brainstorming software, and so forth.

One important capability that must be part of this category is known as discussion software that enables individuals and groups to exchange ideas and hold discussions across the network, thus helping to uncover tacit knowledge. Again, several different products are available on the market for this purpose and the key is to select one that can be implemented throughout the company's entire global IS structure so that no one is excluded from its use.

Discussion software can create a "virtual coffeepot," a place where people with similar interests or problems can "gather" to exchange ideas, to help each other solve problems, and to learn from each other. In the earlier example from Xerox, a discussion area could provide a forum for tech-reps to continue to exchange ideas even when they can't meet in person over the coffeepot. The best discussion-forum software available today includes capabilities for sharing diagrams, video clips, and other types of media that could prove useful for these types of discussions.

There should be no limit on the number of topic areas for discussions nor should there be any restriction on who can participate (although private, limited-access discussion areas may be desirable for groups working on specific projects). In fact, anyone in the company should be allowed to set up his or her own discussion topic either doing it him- or herself or by sending a request to the IS department.

To make discussion forums really useful, follow these rules:

- *Discussions should be monitored.* If you look at the discussion guidelines published by the major Internet service providers, you can read their basic rules for participation in their discussions. Your company should publish its own set of guidelines and monitor the use of the forums to ensure that the guidelines are followed. Figure 8-1 includes the guidelines that we have published for the discussion forums sponsored by Wang Global Virtual University.

Figure 8-1. Wang Global Virtual University's Guidelines for Using Discussion Forums

Participation in the WGVU Learning Exchange is a privilege granted to you based on following appropriate behavior. Please read on for the guidelines you agree to follow as a participant in our discussion forum and chat areas.

ABOUT THE EXCHANGE

The learning exchange area is a community where WGVU students can communicate with other WGVU students. It is a place for students to get answers to questions and courseware support and to chat with other students about the course material. It is also a moderated forum for students to chat with subject matter experts at specified times.

ABOUT OUR MESSAGE FORUMS

WGVU organizes posted messages from our users onto virtual bulletin boards. Messages remain after posting for other users to respond to. We encourage you to read postings at your own pace, take time in composing your messages, and initiate new discussion topics in areas that interest you.

LANGUAGE

WGVU chat and message boards allow you to talk, exchange ideas, and enjoy yourself in the company of other WGVU students from all over the world. Like any community, however, ours only works if we all treat each other with respect. You may not "flame," harass, threaten, or abuse others. Hate speech or language that is racist, obscene, vulgar, or otherwise objectionable is prohibited.

REGISTRATION AND IDENTITY

In WGVU chat and message boards, you must use your full, real name and your real email address when you register with the system.

Discussion areas need to be maintained. Someone needs to be assigned the task of cleaning up old discussions and capturing the vital information within those discussions for placement in the content database. Old or incorrect information should be removed.

Whoever takes the responsibility for monitoring and maintaining each discussion forum should also maintain a list of experts on the topic of discussion. Subject matter experts within the company should be measured on how well they help others learn by answering posted questions. Such intellectual challenges are necessary for the professional growth of even the most knowledgeable professionals in the organization: "The best organizations constantly push their professionals beyond the comfort of their book knowledge, simulation models, and controlled laboratories. They relentlessly drive associates to deal with the more complex intellectual realms of live customers, real operating systems, and high differentiated external environments and cultural differences" (Quinn, Anderson & Finkelstein 1996).

Now that you have a fundamental understanding of the knowledge network, let's talk about how to use the knowledge network to support ISDL.

THE KNOWLEDGE NETWORK AS A SUPPORT TO ISDL

Harvard Business School professor David Garvin (1993) defines a "learning organization" as "an organization skilled at creating, acquiring, and transferring knowledge, and at modifying its behavior to reflect new knowledge and insights." This definition is very compatible with the goals of ISDL as I have described them in this book. Garvin (1993) identifies five "building blocks" for a learning organization:

- systematic problem solving
- experimentation
- learning from past experience
- learning from others
- transferring knowledge.

Next, I will examine how the knowledge network can support each of these building blocks.

Systematic Problem Solving

Many methodologies and tools are available for systematic problem solving. The knowledge network can help people with systematic problem solving by making appropriate tools available and bringing people together in teams to work together, locally or in a distributed fashion, across the network. For example, using the knowledge network, it is possible to hold electronic brainstorming sessions by calling upon people from many different locations around the globe. Bringing those people together physically for a few-hour session would be prohibitively expensive.

Experimentation

Again, the tools available on the knowledge network can facilitate the process of experimentation and the sharing of results of that experimentation. Furthermore, by posting experiments and their results in the content database, a company can reduce duplication of effort. A group in one region may be able to avoid spending unnecessary time, effort, and funds carrying out an experiment when they see that someone else in the company has already tried it. In addition, by using the connections database, an experimenter can find others with similar backgrounds and interests to form a community of practice in which they can share ideas and experiments with others working on the same concepts.

Learning from Past Experience

This is an area where the knowledge network can really shine. The content database helps employees learn from the experiences of other employees. But it will only work if the company and its employees have the discipline needed to record their experiences, both positive and negative. The connections database is also very useful in this regard, for it helps employees make connections to others who have had similar experiences. By using the tools of the knowledge network, employees can then start discussions or dialogues to help uncover the tacit knowledge of those other employees, so that they can better learn from their past experience.

Learning from Others

You can learn from others only if you know who they are and how to find them. The connections and learning-resources databases help you identify other people. The individual and group-learning facilitation tools then can help to provide the means for learning through discussion and dialogue or more structured learning methods.

Transferring Knowledge

This is the reason for the existence of the knowledge network and all of its components: to facilitate the transfer of knowledge, both

Learning from Others' Missteps

When I was a graduate business student, I once took a course entitled "Cases and Studies in Economics and Finance," perhaps the most valuable course in my academic career. One of the case studies was sent to the professor some years earlier by a former student who was very proud of the analysis of a capital investment project he had done for his first employer. Although the student had explained carefully his logic at each of eight decision points, the class's analysis showed that at every decision point, he had made the wrong decision. Nevertheless, upon an initial, cursory examination of the case study, each of us in the class would have come to the same erroneous conclusion. The case study made an outstanding learning experience for our class; it showed us the necessity of careful analysis.

explicit and tacit. At the same time, you should realize that the knowledge network does not contain knowledge, but only data. From the learning model (figure 1-1), you will remember that knowledge comes from applying information to your work. The contents of the knowledge network are all data. The tools of the knowledge network enable you to find the pieces of data that are relevant and purposeful to your work, that is to find information. It is only when you apply that information to your work that you can say that you have mastered it and that you have transformed it into your personal knowledge.

Because the knowledge network can contain only data in the form of words, numbers, diagrams, audio and video segments, and so forth, people can only put their explicit knowledge into the various databases. The connections database enables employees to make the people-to-people connections necessary to start discussion and dialogue—the primary means for transferring tacit knowledge.

THE TRAINING ORGANIZATION'S ROLE IN THE KNOWLEDGE NETWORK

Traditionally, training groups have had little to do with the building of knowledge networks or knowledge-management systems. Knowledge-

All Learning Is Self-Directed

management conferences I have attended seem to be filled with IS professionals with few trainers in evidence. Clearly, IS must be involved in the building of knowledge networks, since knowledge networks rely on technology. Nevertheless, the knowledge network fills a vital role for the training group, especially if the company is moving toward ISDL.

As described throughout this chapter, the knowledge network can be a true enabler and facilitator of ISDL, but to make the knowledge network a real learning tool, the training group must be heavily involved in its design and implementation in the following ways:

- In designing the content database, the training group can use its background in learning theory to identify the types of information that will be most useful in meeting employees' learning needs. The training group should be involved in determining both the composition and structure of the content database to make it an effective learning resource. The training group can also provide instruction to employees on how to use the content database as a learning tool.

- In the design of the connections database, the training group can use its background in competency profiling and assessment to help build its structure. The training group can also help instruct people on how to initially complete and continuously update their individual profiles for the database. Most important, the training group can work with individual employees to teach them how to effectively share their knowledge with others through discussion, dialogue, and the various tools that are available on the network.

- The training group must take primary responsibility for creating and maintaining the learning-resources database. Although there are provisions for all employees to add information to that database, no other group in the company has the expertise for building this directory of learning resources.

- The training group should also be directly involved in deciding which individual and group learning facilitation tools will be included in the network. Maybe you call these database tools, groupware, or other names, but they are all learning tools to help employees find the information they need from the knowledge network.

- The training group must teach employees at all levels how to use the knowledge network as a necessary means for implementing ISDL.

Employees must learn how to contribute to the knowledge network, how to search it for information or contacts they need, how to use the information they find, how to work with the people they locate, how to use the various tools to learn, and how to apply their learning to their work to move toward their individual and collective goals. No other group in the company can do this, and ISDL cannot become a reality in the company without this assistance.

LEARNING ASSIGNMENT

Is there a knowledge-management initiative taking place anywhere in your company? Does your organization have a chief knowledge officer? If so, contact those responsible and find out as much as you can about the knowledge initiative.

Suggest ways in which the training group can add value to the knowledge-management effort. Organize a brainstorming session with representatives from the knowledge-management group, the training group, and the target audience for the knowledge-management initiative.

To inventory your company's knowledge-management initiatives and then to discover ways in which the training group can complement those initiatives, consider the following:

- Which knowledge-management initiatives are underway?
- Who heads up the initiative?
- Who else in the company is involved in the initiative?

- Is there any relationship between this initiative and the efforts of the training group? If so, describe how they complement each other or compete with each other.

- How could the training group add value to this knowledge-management initiative? Alternatively, how could the knowledge-management initiative add value to specific training programs?

- Who has the ability to form a coalition between the knowledge-management and the training group to help both those groups and the company as a whole make better use of learning resources within the company?

- Develop a strategy for getting the two groups to work together.

Chapter 9

Growing and Sustaining an Independent Learning Culture

The previous chapters of this book were dedicated to introducing ISDL; describing PLEs in which learning can take place; establishing the roles of employees, managers, and company leaders in ISDL; scoping the modes of technology-based training; and presenting the concept of a knowledge network. Each chapter included recommendations for moving toward successful implementation of ISDL. In this chapter, I consolidate these recommendations in the form of checklists and expand upon them. Here I will show you how to move beyond the ideas and scenarios presented throughout the book and do something positive with them starting *today*. As you embark on the journey to ISDL, consider that three factors can make the difference between success and failure for the movement to ISDL. Companies must

- help employees get started in using the new ISDL methods
- assist employees as they learn to share their own knowledge and skills with each other
- align corporate measurements and rewards with the new learning methods.

GETTING ISDL OFF THE GROUND

Unlike the baseball field in the film *Field of Dreams,* it is not necessarily true that "if you build it, they will come." Too often companies
make this incorrect assumption, and the introduction of ISDL is a
flop. The to-do list for companies that wish to initiate ISDL is a long
one: build a PLE, catalyze changes in the behavior of leaders and managers, and invest in building the company's knowledge network. Yet,
five essential factors remain:

- Employees must know about the learning resources available
to them.
- Employees must have easy access to those resources.
- Employees must have the tools to use those resources readily
available, and they must know how to use those tools.
- Employees must have the time needed to undertake the needed
learning.
- Employees must be willing to help each other learn.

Publicizing ISDL

Checklist

- ☐ Sell ISDL.
- ☐ Get everybody on board with CBT.
- ☐ Create special publicity materials.
- ☐ Give incentives.
- ☐ Publish success stories.

Sell ISDL. You have to sell your training programs to employees. The
best salespeople are the employees' direct managers. At Wang Global,
the employees who make the best and most rapid progress through
the training are those who report that their managers continually ask
them how the training is going and emphasize how important the
training is to the company, their group, and to their individual careers.

Joyce Douglass (1999) of Science Application International Corporation (SAIC) uses a number of strategies to publicize and sell her group's CBT programs. For example, SAIC's training group held a number of open houses to publicize the training. Although this is not possible to do in every work location, especially when some worksites have just a few employees and if worksites are scattered across the globe, it should be possible in the company's major locations. "Food is a great attractor," she says. "We hold [open houses] at lunchtime with free food and door prizes."

Get everybody on board with CBT. The process of getting everybody up to speed with CBT helps publicize the programs to those who might not get the word from the Website or email. Many employees who don't use personal computers regularly may be lost when it comes to accessing and using the courseware and may be too embarrassed to ask for help. You need to teach them the ropes for accessing and downloading the course, and this is a conduit for reaching these people who might otherwise be out of the loop for electronic publicity. I can attest to the viability of this solution: The training manager at Wang Global's large call center in Houston, Texas, invited me to hold a number of "how-to" sessions on WGVU programs with employees and managers. Because of half-dozen sessions I held during two trips there, the Houston facility has some of the highest participation rates and completion rates of any Wang Global facility.

Create special publicity materials. Get posters, coffee mugs, and banners made up—whatever it takes to keep the training programs in front of employees' eyes and minds. At Wang Global, we provide every student with a mouse pad emblazoned with the WGVU logo. When Buckman Laboratories started its knowledge network and discussion forums, they distributed a poster that showed Caesar standing in front of the Roman Senate with the caption, "Caesar had his forum, now you have yours" (Tobin 1997).

Give incentives. Even when a company makes a major effort to move many of its training and learning activities to ISDL, an important role still exists for instructor-led training, especially on more advanced topics and where the classroom experience cannot be matched by ISDL. Given the relative scarcity of these types of events, they tend to become even more popular. By making ISDL a prerequisite to attendance at these events, you can provide a real incentive to complete the necessary ISDL programs.

Publish success stories. Wary learners will learn of and be encouraged by hearing of others' success. Publicize learning stories in the company newsletter, on learning Websites, and in the company's annual report. Invite professional and industry journals and magazines to write stories about the company's ISDL efforts and have the writers interview line employees rather than high-level managers. Take every opportunity to publicize your programs inside and outside the company.

Wang Global's Multifaceted Approach to "Sell" Training

When Wang Global Virtual University was introduced, we used many different strategies to publicize the programs. We launched WGVU with a special ceremony that we videotaped. It included presentations from our CEO and several company vice presidents and a live online chat session to answer employee questions. The videotape was distributed as part of a quarterly communication package sent to managers throughout the company. We created an announcement that was sent by email to every company employee. Announcements of the programs were the lead articles in *IntraWang,* the company newsletter. Stories about WGVU, its programs, and students were included in each quarterly newsletter. Later, I started writing a regular column for the newsletter to track the progress of the programs. We created our own Website both to publicize the program and to provide access to courseware and other learning resources.

Nevertheless, this barrage of publicity wasn't enough. For months, we still received calls from employees saying that they "heard something about training" and wanted to get more information. We learned more than a few lessons about publicizing ISDL.

We learned that not everyone reads corporate email announcements or the company newsletter. Also, you can't publicize a Website solely through the Website. If employees aren't accustomed to surfing the Web, and if they don't regularly use the company's intranet, they aren't going to find the training Website. Even if they do find it, they won't know how to use it.

I also made a number of presentations at quarterly meetings of field managers for some of the company's major lines of business. The purpose of these meetings was twofold: to publicize our programs and to answer managers' questions and concerns about the program.

What more could we have done to promote our programs? I believe that our biggest mistake was in our failure to get out to the field to hold more information sessions, open houses, and demonstrations for employees.

Learning to Use ISDL

Checklist
☐ Teach the basics.
☐ Form study groups.
☐ Make sure everyone's computer skills are up to par.

Teach the basics. Employees who have never used ISDL before, whether it involves starting a CD-ROM-based program on their PC, downloading a CBT course from a server, or participating in a Web-based conference, may be hesitant to display their ignorance of how to do these things. Joyce Douglass (1999) reports that SAIC publishes a desktop-reference manual and gives demonstrations at open houses to allow people to learn without having to ask for help. Also, SAIC asks current users to help other employees get started. Joyce Douglass calls this approach "facilitated CBT," whereby one employee coaches another through the CBT program.

Form study groups. In some companies, employees form study groups with or without the aid of the training group so that they can coach each other during the learning experience. Often, the study group will ask a more experienced employee to meet with them periodically to answer questions and offer guidance on learning paths.

Make sure everyone's computer skills are up to par. What is clear is that ISDL is a new learning method for many people, especially when it comes to the use of technology-based or technology-facilitated learning programs. Just because every employee in the company has a PC and uses it in the normal course of business does not mean that he or she will automatically know how to use it for learning purposes. It may seem to be a contradiction to say that you need to hold instructor-led classes to teach people how to learn on their own, but it is often a necessary step in introducing ISDL into a company.

Training People How to Use Email

Most companies today use email but few train people on how to use it. Most assume that people have always used email and will pick it up naturally. Consider, though, how much junk email and poorly written email you receive every day.

Elliott Masie (1999b), of the Masie Center, performed an informal survey of participants in one of the Center's programs. He notes, "Few organizations . . . had any programs aimed at teaching people HOW to use email. As the most widely used computer application in most organizations, who is setting the tone and process for corporate communication? What is the protocol for dealing with low-priority email during high stress times?"

If companies aren't training people on how to use email properly, the chances are they are paying even less attention to training their employees on how to use knowledge networks and ISDL programs.

Making the Tools Available

Checklist

- ❑ Evaluate hardware and software availability and capabilities.
- ❑ Consider a PC loaner program.
- ❑ Consider interest-free loans to employees for computers.
- ❑ Create training in alternative formats.

Evaluate hardware and software availability and capabilities. Make certain that employees have the equipment they need to use the training materials and that equipment has the right tools and the required capacity. If ISDL programs are provided on CD-ROM, make certain that the employee's personal computer has a CD-ROM drive or provide the right equipment in a local study center.

Consider a PC loaner program. Some companies loan PCs to employees who want to study at home but lack a properly configured PC. Other companies provide a lending library of CD-ROMs and other learning materials so employees can take them home if they wish.

Consider interest-free loans to employees for computers. Some employees may need to buy computers for learning at home. Companies can set up programs to assist employees with financing computer purchases. Payments can be made via payroll deduction. At some companies, the loan for the computer equipment is forgiven if the employee successfully completes a specific training program. Some also reimburse employees for the monthly cost of signing up with an Internet service provider.

Create training in alternative formats. Another company found that audiotapes were a popular learning method for salespeople, because they could listen to the tapes as they drove from one customer site to another. Although having a cassette player in the salespeople's company cars was formerly considered an unnecessary luxury, the newest fleet was ordered with cassette players to facilitate the use of this learning method. Other options to consider are printed materials, Website access, and traditional instructor-led training. Another example is Dell Computer, which is also training many employees to become MCSEs and MCSDs. They give their employees many options for training, including books, classroom training, and CBT.

Versatility is the Key at Wang Global

At Wang Global, we tried to make as much of our Microsoft certification training as possible available from our intranet Website. Although most of our employees/students were able to access the courseware from this site, we also had to make other accommodations.

(continued on next page)

Growing and Sustaining an Independent Learning Culture   159

Versatility is the Key at Wang Global *(continued)*

For example, some employees just prefer to study from books, rather from the CBT courseware—our primary training strategy. Our policy is that if they want to study from books, we will provide the books. We had two employees in Singapore who traveled to and from work on a two-hour train ride. Using books and these four hours of study time each day, they helped each other achieve certification within six months. In another case, we had an employee who could not use books or CBT programs because of dyslexia. In that case, we authorized him to take classes from a Microsoft training center. We also had to make special accommodations for some employees who encountered challenges regarding network bandwidth and firewall-access problems (chapter 7).

The point is that no single solution is going to meet everyone's learning needs, so the training group has to be flexible in its approaches.

Making Time for Learning

Checklist

☐ Make learning part of the job description.

☐ Determine the amount of study time necessary.

☐ Allocate time for learning.

☐ Negotiate a study schedule.

☐ Set aside space for learning.

☐ Set aside time for learning.

Make learning part of the job description. For ISDL to work, the company must create a learning environment where learning is an integral part of every employee's job description. Although many companies pride themselves on giving every employee 40 or more hours of formal training every year, learning cannot be so bounded. Learning takes time, and time must be allocated to the employee for learning.

Although learning takes place in many informal ways, such as attending meetings, conversing with other employees in person, via email, or through a discussion forum, there must still be time allocated for formal learning activities.

Determine the amount of study time necessary. Examine the ISDL program to estimate how much time the employees will need to complete it. Remember that employees who are less computer-savvy may need more time than those who use computers frequently. Just because an employee doesn't need to be away from work for one or more days to attend an instructor-led program does not mean that zero time is required for training. In some future scenario, if companies start implanting chips into people's heads and then plug them into the corporate network, companies will be able to instantaneously download the knowledge and skills needed by employees, but this solution exists today only in science fiction.

Allocate time for learning. When a company changes the format of a training program from instructor-led to ISDL, it is saving on travel time and expenses associated with bringing employees to a central or regional training location. At the same time, employees still need to allocate the time necessary to learn the new material, to gain the new knowledge, or build the new skill. Too often, I have seen companies eliminate a weeklong, instructor-led training program, put all of the material on videotape or CD-ROM, and expect employees to go through the material on their own time. It rarely works.

Once you have converted everything to a self-paced format, you still have to allow time for learning activities. Although CBT and other self-paced formats offer the possibility of reducing training time (as compared to instructor-led training), the reduction is not 100 percent. You need to allocate some part of the employee's work time to structured study time.

Negotiate a study schedule. You and the employee need to establish a fair division between company and personal time for training. It is usually reasonable to ask employees to use some of their own time to study if the ISDL program is designed to help their career advancement, but if it is strictly a requirement for his or her current work, the time should come from the normal workday. Some companies have successfully negotiated a 50-50 split with employees: "We'll allow you to take one day from your work schedule to study if you take one day from your own time for the same purpose."

Set aside space for learning. When you release employees from work for study purposes, make certain that they can really use that time. Send them to study centers where they won't be disturbed by telephone calls or computers that chime whenever new email arrives. Have someone else cover telephone duty during study periods. If there is no study center, create a sign (figure 9-1) that they can hang on doors or workspace entrances. Employees can also use the signs at home to let family members know that they need a dedicated space and time for learning activities.

Set aside time for learning. If we don't set aside time for learning activities, if we try to squeeze learning in among many other tasks, our learning may be compromised. Elliott Masie has held several hour-long briefings over telephone and Internet connections with hundreds of participants. In a recent newsletter, he mused about whether participants' focus was really on the briefing:

Figure 9-1. Sign to indicate that learning is ongoing within.

All Learning Is Self-Directed

Can we multitask and learn? As learning becomes more available at the desktop, in the cubicle and office, we will have to confront the up and down sides of learner multitasking. Over the past few months, I have facilitated about 1,300 people participating in a range of real-time learning events, using a combination of telephones and Web collaborative interfaces. I have had the sense that a large percentage of these folks, who voluntarily signed up for these one-hour short briefings, were doing a bit of multitasking. Check the email, surf to an intranet page, take a phone call on the other line or other easy-to-do second tasks in the midst of my "deeply engaging interactive lecture" (Masie 1999a).

HELPING EACH OTHER LEARN

Checklist

- ❏ Change the "cheating" mentality.
- ❏ Bring people together for learning.
- ❏ Model knowledge-sharing behaviors.
- ❏ Move toward a self-managing, high-performance organization.
- ❏ Give the changes time to take hold in the organizational culture.

Encourage openness to sharing learning. Moving to ISDL does not necessarily mean that each employee in the organization will learn alone. In fact, much of the learning you do every day on the job relies on other people sharing their knowledge with you in either a structured or unstructured way. When you ask someone how to fill out a company-required form, when you seek out a colleague to show you how to perform a function on a spreadsheet program, when you listen to other people talking about their work over lunch, you are learning. You rely on others to help you learn, and so you should be willing to share your own knowledge and skills with others. Openness to sharing knowledge is a basic prerequisite for the successful movement to ISDL in any company.

Change the "cheating" mentality. If "knowledge is power," how do we convince employees to share their power with others? Even in today's booming economy, mergers and acquisitions result in many layoffs. Conventional thinking goes, "If I have business-critical knowledge that no one else in the company has, then the merged company or my company's new owners won't dare to lay me off." Many such conventional thinkers find themselves back in the job market. The new thinking goes something like this: "If I am known as a valuable knowledge asset, that I not only have a great store of knowledge, but I openly share my knowledge with others so that many people and the company as a whole benefits, then my value to the company will be clear."

Knowledge is a unique type of economic good. With most economic goods, if you give them away, you no longer possess them. With knowledge, you can give it away and still keep it. In fact, the more you share your knowledge, the greater its value. Unfortunately, at least in most Western societies, we are not raised to share our knowledge with others. Although the trend appears to be changing, we are not allowed to share our knowledge with others throughout our school years—it is called cheating. Only in the past decade or two has there been a trend toward encouraging teamwork in the classroom at all levels from elementary school through graduate education.

Bring people together for learning. Independent, self-directed learning does not necessarily mean learning in isolation. In fact, people need at least some personal contact with each other to learn most effectively, despite the many technological tools available for maintaining electronic connections. Kimball and Mareen Fisher (1999) report, "Hewlett-Packard's new-product design teams find that it is also important to avoid creating a culture where personal contact is shunned in lieu of only virtual interaction. Hewlett Packard, Levi Strauss & Company, and numerous other companies that use people from all over the world for special project assignments confirm that

Bringing the Group Together Under One Roof

When I worked for Digital Equipment Corporation, we did a study of a product development team that included employees from several different locations in the United States and from several European countries. One finding of the study was that to make the team work well together across large distances, electronic support tools were vital. We found that an even more vital factor was bringing the team together for the first 30 to 60 days so that the team members could get to know each other. Without this personal knowledge, the electronic communications among team members over the next two years would have been much more difficult and much less effective.

For example, team members got used to one engineer's abrupt style of writing email. Without knowing the individual, the engineer's terse replies might have offended others on the team. By getting to know the individual, team members knew that he was a valuable member of the team who liked and respected team members, but who "couldn't be bothered with writing chatty email messages."

---

some things—especially project kick-offs, sensitive feedback sessions, and certain brainstorming activities—can only be done face-to-face."

Model knowledge-sharing behaviors. As stated in earlier chapters, leaders who model knowledge-sharing behaviors, through mentoring and coaching other employees, can set the organizational climate for learning. Consultant Lynda McDermott (1999) puts it this way: "The best leaders coach, and the best coaches receive some coaching themselves. Although no leader can guarantee success, whether that be a Super Bowl victory or record year-end profits, those who demonstrate a willingness and ability to coach certainly better the odds."

Move toward a self-managing, high-performance organization. Having employees share knowledge with each other is a prerequisite for individual and organizational learning. When you turn responsibility for learning over to the employees, you are asking them to manage themselves, the first step to a self-managing, high-performance organization. Nevertheless, self-managing organizations must take responsibility for both individual and organizational learning. Ronald Purser (1999) says it this way: "In essence, self-managing organizations are designed so people can learn from their mistakes and correct problems in real time: they are flexible, error-reducing systems. They are designed to allow people to operate in an optimal zone of performance, within a dynamic equilibrium: not chained to a rigid order at one extreme, nor falling into a black hole of chaos and anarchy at the other, but at a higher order of complexity, which is what self-managing organizations are all about."

Give the changes time to take hold in the organizational culture. Because sharing one's knowledge is not the accepted cultural norm in most societies or most companies, we need to find ways of encouraging people to share their knowledge with others. The good news is that sharing knowledge can become addictive; once you get started using tools like a knowledge network, you won't ever want to live without those tools again. In companies like Buckman Laboratories, where there is a large, well-utilized knowledge network, employees would be lost today if the knowledge network were to disappear. As much publicity as Buckman has received on its knowledge network, leaders of their effort are quick to point out that it took about five years of effort to get the network and the culture of the company to the point where people considered its use a normal part of their jobs and a decade to get to its current state (Tobin 1997).

ALIGNING MEASUREMENTS AND REWARDS WITH ISDL

Nothing has sunk more corporate change efforts than the misalignment of corporate measurement and reward systems: If you want people to move to new behaviors, you cannot continue to measure and reward them on the basis of old behaviors. How can companies use their measurement and reward systems to promote ISDL?

Use learning contracts for employees. Require the learning contract (figure 4-1) to be a regular part of every employee's job plan and review process. Tie some portion of individual compensation to learning objectives, as specified in the individual's learning contract.

Offer incentives to those who share learning. Measure employees on how much they use the knowledge network to learn and to share their knowledge and experience with others. Give rewards to employees who teach others, either through holding classes (live or technology-mediated) or coaching and mentoring others in the company. Rewards don't always have to be monetary. A special luncheon with the company's CEO can often provide greater motivation than a small bonus payment.

Evaluate how well managers foster ISDL and the knowledge network. Measure managers in part on how much time they spend coaching and mentoring their employees. Gauge how managers follow up with employees about their learning. See if managers are learning with and from their employees. Ensure that managers model desirable learning behaviors.

✓ Recognize those who apply ISDL to their jobs. Start a "Learner of the Month" award to be given to the employee who has improved job performance or solved some longstanding group or company problem through ISDL. Form an ISDL Council to advise the company on its ISDL strategy and policies. The council should comprise individuals who are recognized as outstanding learners—those who have undertaken ISDL and then applied their learning to their jobs to make real differences in business results. If the company receives an invitation to speak at a conference about its ISDL activities, suggest as the speaker an employee who has effectively used ISDL, rather than a person from the training group or a high-level HR manager.

✓ Encourage users of the knowledge network. Hold special events for the top users of the company's knowledge network. For example, at Buckman Laboratories, the chairman held a special event at a golf resort in Scottsdale, Arizona, for the top users of the knowledge network. The program featured a number of prestigious speakers. Daily email reports on happenings at the event sparked even greater interest among those employees who were not invited. As a result, many who had not been using the knowledge network started doing so, if only to avoid missing out on future events (Tobin 1997).

✓ Reward actions that forestall problems. Too often have companies recognized some individual heroic effort with an award or other reward, when the crisis that the person overcame would never have happened had the person learned more about what the company had done in the past or in other locations. Companies tend to give greater rewards to people who come up with solutions on their own than to those who find applicable solutions elsewhere. The "manager as fire fighter" is not the right paradigm for today's and tomorrow's business. Rather, employees should be rewarded for "fire prevention"—for averting crises that would require heroic action. Furthermore, they should be rewarded for solving problems, whether or not the solution came from their own minds or from somewhere else. In fact, if you want to maximize the utilization of the vast store of company knowledge, employees should be given greater rewards for applying existing solutions that work than for spending their time inventing new solutions.

GROWING AND MANAGING AN INDEPENDENT LEARNING CULTURE

Too many companies have viewed a movement to ISDL as a one-time event. Perhaps the training budget was getting too large, so the CEO mandated that the training group be reduced or abolished and everything be moved to an ISDL format. As I have already argued, you cannot move "everything" to an ISDL format—it just doesn't work for some subjects. It is estimated that today 70 percent of all corporate training occurs in the classroom; most of the other 30 percent occurs in an ISDL format. My prediction is that within the next decade, we will get to a 50-50 mix of instructor-led and ISDL instruction. Although improvements in technology may make technology-based instruction much more common, it will not eliminate the need to have an instructor or other knowledgeable learning facilitator leading some instruction.

Moving to ISDL does not mean that you can convert a formerly instructor-led course to some self-paced format and believe that the new self-paced materials will last forever. Even with instructor-led training, many companies' training catalogs are still filled with obsolete courses and methods. It is much easier to create a new learning program than to retire it. Just as the company's business will change over time, so will the learning needs of the company's employees. Just as the technologies used in the company's business will change, so will the technologies used for instruction. Even if you transform the majority of the company's training programs to a self-paced format, you will still need to have a training group to maintain those programs, update them, and create new programs in response to the needs of the business and its employees.

When your company finds the right mix of instructor-led courses and ISDL, when the training group has expanded its repertoire of methods and services to include the facilitation of ISDL along with traditional training methods, and when you have built a PLE that extends from the board room to the factory floor to even the most remote sales or service location, you will find that this new environment will be self-sustaining. Employees will stay with your company because they are constantly challenged in their work and because they are always learning and growing. Your company will find eager applicants for new positions in the company because of the new culture and working/learning environment. Your company will find that its business results, both in terms of return on equity and return on intellectual capital, are moving in the right direction.

This all requires a concerted focus on learning as a core value of the company, a focus that must be nurtured and maintained. Just as no company today can state that its current set of products or services will carry it through the next decade, neither can a company say that its current stock of knowledge and skills is all it will ever need. In today's global economy, the intellectual capital of a company, the knowledge and skills of the organization and its employees, is its only source of sustainable competitive advantage. As is true for physical capital, intellectual capital must be maintained and renewed.

KEEPING THE ORGANIZATION FOCUSED ON INDEPENDENT LEARNING

When learning activities become central to the achievement of the company's business objectives, it will be easy to keep the company focused on learning. In many companies, even if the CEO maintains a sharp focus on learning, it doesn't mean that that focus will extend to managers at all levels of the company. That is why leadership for learning is so vital to the success of ISDL.

In presentations that I give frequently on evaluating training programs, I argue against ever doing an ROI calculation for training programs. I also advise against using traditional smile sheets that many training organizations continue to use to evaluate their programs. When audience members ask me how I measure the success of my own training organization, I reply, "If the company is successful, and if I hear business leaders are remarking, 'We couldn't have been this successful if not for the efforts of the training organization,' then my training organization has been successful."

In successful companies where ISDL is part of an overall learning strategy and where company leaders have built and continue to maintain a PLE, learning will be self-sustaining.

Meeting Wang Global's Business Goals via Training and Certification

One of the things that most surprised me about Wang Global's partnership agreement with Microsoft was the level of interest in Wang Global's training numbers among stock analysts and institutional investors. These Wall-Street types, who traditionally focus solely on earnings statements and balance sheets, were now asking to review our training and certification numbers. The company's CEO and chief financial officer were not only reporting the training and certification numbers in their quarterly conference calls with the analysts and investors, but putting them at the top of the agenda! It would seem that on Wall Street, the focus in company evaluations is shifting from investments in physical capital to, at least in part, investments in human capital.

LEARNING ASSIGNMENT

In essence, this entire chapter was a learning assignment. The checklists highlight the tasks involved in moving your company toward successful ISDL. Review the checklists and evaluate how far your company has come and which tasks still remain. Consider the following:

- How effective is your group at promoting ISDL?
- How do you encourage knowledge sharing among employees and quash the "cheating" mentality?
- How do you reward those who share knowledge, apply their learning at the worksite, and, most important, those who are "fire preventers" instead of "fire fighters"?

Chapter 10

Future of ISDL in the Workplace

In this chapter, I will present a scenario to demonstrate the power of ISDL in helping a company and an individual employee meet their respective business goals. Finally, the chapter will conclude with a discussion of the potential power of ISDL in the workplace of the future.

WINNING THE BUSINESS OF CHEMGLOBAL[*]

Bob Smith is a newly hired sales representative for ProConsul Advisory Services, a large consulting firm. His first assignment is to win the company's first major business with ChemGlobal, a multinational chemical firm with headquarters in the region he covers. The firm has never worked with anyone from company headquarters, and Bob has no knowledge of the company or its key employees, but he has, in a previous job, sold services to one of the target company's competitors.

---

[*]All names of people and organizations are fictitious.

In this chapter, I will describe Bob's learning experiences as he uncovers information about the company, its essential employees, and its major challenges. Bob will develop a strategy and plan to win the company's business.

Bob has been through ProConsul's basic sales-training program and has learned about its knowledge network and its library of learning resources. Now, he sits down at his PC and logs on. He then calls up his Web browser and goes to the knowledge-network homepage on the company's intranet. On the learning-resources page, he clicks on the "chemical industry knowledge pack" icon to download the pack to his PC. This is one of many industry "knowledge packs" developed by ProConsul's training group. It contains basic information on the chemical industry, its structure, listings of players in the industry, various types of industry rankings, a glossary of essential terms, and short descriptions of major projects that the company has undertaken for customers in that industry. Bob reads the basic information in the knowledge pack and sees that there is no mention of ChemGlobal in the listing of the firm's major projects. He then spends the rest of the day reviewing the industry profile and the list of other chemical industry projects the firm has undertaken. He begins taking notes about the types of capabilities that the firm has that might apply to ChemGlobal.

Later that day, Bob returns to the learning-resources database and clicks on the "news service" icon. He starts by entering a search for news items and articles on ChemGlobal for the past two years. He checks off the news sources—general business and industry-specific— that he wants to search. As he enters the search, he is asked if he wants to subscribe to the news service so that future articles on Chem-Global from those same sources will be sent to him by email as they appear. He clicks "yes."

The news-service search yields 147 articles. He scrolls through the abstracts of the articles, checking off those that he wants to save for future reference. After selecting and saving 41 articles, he prints out 10 of them to read overnight. He also goes into a financial database to retrieve ChemGlobal's last three annual reports, copies of their last three years' 10-K reports, and a listing of current officers and saves them all on his PC. He also prints out recent reports on ChemGlobal done by three major brokerage houses.

Before signing off for the day, he goes to the homepage for the ProConsul's "content database" and does a search for the ChemGlobal name. The search returns three items: a small logistics project done for ChemGlobal's Malaysian plant several years ago and two losing proposals that ProConsul had written for foreign subsidiaries of Chem-Global last year. Bob makes a note of the project manager's name, and he prints out a summary of the two unsuccessful proposals. He also prints out the postmortem analyses done by the proposal teams on why ProConsul didn't win the business and also notes the names of the proposal managers and the firm's partner who was responsible for each proposal.

Bob spends much of his evening and most of the next day reading all of the information he has gathered on ChemGlobal. He writes his own profile of the company, including its strengths and weaknesses, latest innovations, and how it stacks up against its own industry competitors. He jots down potential areas of opportunity for ProConsul Advisory Services. Along with his written profile, he is forming his own mental picture of the firm and generating ideas on how best to approach some of its main officers.

Once he has completed this review, Bob goes into the content database and does a search for major projects done for ChemGlobal's competitors. While he reads the abstracts of all 81 of ProConsul's projects done in the chemical industry in the last five years, he focuses on a dozen projects done over the past two years that relate to the opportunity areas he has identified. He prints out the original proposals and project reports for those projects and notes the names of the lead consultants on each of the projects.

After lunch, Bob goes back to the knowledge network's homepage and clicks on the icon for the connections database. He does a search of the database using ChemGlobal as the keyword. What he gets back are the names of the following ProConsul staff:

- a junior consultant who had interned with ChemGlobal two summers earlier

- a ProConsul division comptroller in Germany who had been hired from ChemGlobal

- a ProConsul partner in San Francisco who is on the board of directors of a local hospital—a board upon which a director of ChemGlobal also sits.

Bob spends the rest of the week reviewing all of the learning materials he has gathered and working on his ideas on how to approach ChemGlobal. When he finishes, he has 20 pages of notes, but he has a lingering feeling that he has missed something important. He realizes that although he has learned a lot about ChemGlobal and its competitors, he hasn't done much research on general trends in the chemical industry. He signs back on to the learning-resources database and finds a half-dozen recent articles relating to the chemical industry and the potential areas of opportunity he has identified. He updates his notes and feels that he has put in a good week's work. He'll sleep on the problem over the weekend and present what he has done to his sales manager on Monday morning.

Over the weekend, Bob tries to relax, but ChemGlobal keeps popping into his mind. Three or four times, he stops what he is doing to make a few notes about his new ideas.

On Monday morning, Bob meets with Claire Stephens, his manager, to review his progress on the background research. She is very pleased with his progress, but she suggests, "Bob, I think it's time to contact some of the people on your list—the ones who did the losing proposals for ChemGlobal and the ones who have been winning business with some of ChemGlobal's competitors. It also wouldn't hurt to talk with Amy Weingarten, the local woman who interned with ChemGlobal. I hear that they have a great internship program for people working on their master's degree in business and that they give their interns a great deal of exposure to the company's top officers. Even though she's pretty green, I hear that she is very sharp. In the meantime, I'll contact our partner in San Francisco to see if she knows the ChemGlobal director well enough to get us some introductions and a meeting. I'll also send a note to our partner in Houston, who has a lot of experience working with other companies in the chemical industry. Nice work, Bob. Let's meet again on Thursday at four o'clock."

Bob returns to his office and his PC. He puts together a list of people to contact (table 10-1). After completing the list, he's very impressed with ProConsul's knowledge network. Thinking back to the firm he recently left to take the job at ProConsul Advisory Services, he realizes that it would have taken him at least a month of research (instead of a week) to do this background research and develop a similar list of names, and he probably wouldn't have found half the people he needed to contact. He then writes an email and sends it to the people on his list, finding that two of the people on the list are no longer with the firm. In the email, he introduces himself, talks about the challenge before him, gives a very brief overview of the research he has done, and invites them to join him in a discussion of the possibilities for making a bid to ChemGlobal.

Bob then goes back to the intranet to the "learning facilitators" page on the knowledge network and clicks on the button, "create discussion." He is then prompted for a conference title and a list of names he wants to authorize to use the conference. After entering the list, the system generates and sends an email message to each person asking if they want to participate in the discussion. If they click on "yes," the system will generate an icon on their desktop PC that links them directly to the ChemGlobal discussion forum. Bob then prepares a summary of his research and his ideas and posts them onto the ChemGlobal discussion forum for the other members of the discussion group to review.

While he waits for others to add their comments to the discussion, Bob goes back into the learning-resources database. During his initial sales training, Bob received an overview of the various areas of practice within ProConsul Advisory Services. He had been told that there were short, self-paced training modules in the database that gave more detail on each area of practice, along with some short case studies of typical projects. Bob downloads three of these modules, which correspond to his ideas for ChemGlobal. He spends a few hours on each one, making notes on how he might apply the ideas to an eventual ChemGlobal proposal. He also notes that there are references to other tools on the knowledge network that will help him structure the proposal and estimate its cost.

Within 48 hours, Bob has heard back from all but one of the people on his list. From that person, he received an email auto-reply saying

Table 10-1. Initial members of the ChemGlobal discussion forum.

MEMBER	ROLE
Bob Smith	Sales representative with responsibility for winning new business from ChemGlobal
Claire Stephens	Bob's sales manager
Ruth Goldberg	ProConsul partner in San Francisco who serves on a local hospital's board of directors with one of ChemGlobal's board members
Dick James	ProConsul partner in Houston who has in-depth knowledge of the chemical industry
Mary Howard	Local ProConsul partner and Claire Stephens' manager
Heinz Mann	Comptroller for ProConsul in Germany who had previously worked for ChemGlobal
Amy Weingarten	Local junior consultant who had interned at ChemGlobal headquarters
Proposal manager and partner in charge	Submitted the two losing proposals made to ChemGlobal over the past two years
ProConsul's lead consultants	Worked on the dozen projects that Bob had identified as being similar to the areas of opportunity he has identified for the ChemGlobal bid
ProConsul's partners in charge	Practice in the three areas of opportunity that Bob has identified

that he is on vacation for the next two weeks. With those messages he has received three more suggestions for other ProConsul employees to add to the distribution list for the discussion forum. Bob sends them each an invitation to join the forum along with a copy of the original email message; he then adds their names to the authorized list for the discussion forum.

When he next checks the ChemGlobal discussion forum, he finds notes and comments from many of the participants:

- Ruth Goldberg, the partner in San Francisco, says that she will be happy to meet with the ChemGlobal director who she knows to test the waters and to get some contacts, but she wants to wait until Bob has done more homework.

- Mary Howard, the local ProConsul Advisory Services partner, says that she has met Frank Chu, ChemGlobal's chief operating officer, at a meeting of the local university's business-school-advisory board and can arrange a meeting when Bob is ready.

- Heinz Mann, ProConsul Advisory Services comptroller in the Germany office, says that he knows Andre Martin, ChemGlobal's chief financial officer (CFO). He also knows that the CFO recently cancelled a $2 million, three-year contract with one of ProConsul Advisory Services' competitors after the first six months because it wasn't yielding the promised results. He said that he would try to find out what the contract covered and why ChemGlobal was dissatisfied.

- Amy Weingarten, the local consultant, says that she worked in the CFO's office during her ChemGlobal internship and recently had lunch with Betty Clinton, ChemGlobal's treasurer.

- The proposal manager for one of the losing proposals submitted to ChemGlobal said that ProConsul Advisory Services had put together a good proposal but had been underbid by a small, local firm.

- The proposal manager for the other losing proposal was one of those who had left the company. The partner with responsibility for that proposal said that they lost because it was a poor proposal, leading to the dismissal of the proposal manager.

- The lead consultants from the dozen proposals done for other chemical companies contributed bits of intelligence. The most useful contribution came from one consultant who described a new methodology developed by his practice area. It focused on one of the opportunity areas that Bob had identified and had been very successful in two large, pharmaceutical-industry projects.

- Another of those consultants had recently attended a conference and had a tape of a speech made by ChemGlobal's vice president of worldwide manufacturing. He summarized the speech and attached an audio file with a 15-minute segment of the speech from a tape he got from the conference producer.

This was great from Bob's point of view. He thought back to his old firm; he never would have been able to even find most of these people without ProConsul's knowledge network. He is also very impressed and grateful that everyone is so willing to share their knowledge and help him out although it might not directly affect their local business or their own productivity measurements.

At Thursday's meeting with Claire, Bob reviews the progress he has made. Claire is impressed and says that it is time to start making some high-level contacts at ChemGlobal. She asks Bob to prepare a five-page prospectus, summarizing what he has learned and the areas where he thinks that ProConsul Advisory Services might have the greatest opportunities to win business from ChemGlobal. She will present this to Mary Howard, the local partner, and ask for a strategy meeting.

Bob works on the prospectus over the weekend, using a template he found in the tools section of the knowledge network and sends it by email to Claire early Monday morning. By noon, Claire completes some minor editing and forwards the prospectus with a request for a meeting to Mary Howard and Bob. By the end of the day, Mary replies, setting the meeting for Wednesday morning.

While waiting for the Wednesday meeting, Bob continues to monitor the ChemGlobal discussion forum. Heinz Martin reports that he conversed with ChemGlobal's CFO Andre Martin and that the contract, which ChemGlobal recently cancelled with one of ProConsul Advisory Services' competitors, was in one of the opportunity areas that Bob had identified. The reason for the cancellation was that the consulting firm came back after four months of work and told the project sponsor that it would require three years, rather than two, and would cost an extra $1.5 million over the original bid. Ruth Goldberg reports that she had a very brief conversation with the ChemGlobal director at a hospital fundraiser. He said that the CEO is under pressure from the board to improve the performance of the company's Canadian division or to sell it.

Since ChemGlobal's CFO and chief operating officer (COO) seem to be probable contacts for ProConsul Advisory Services, Bob uses some of the search tools available on the knowledge network to gather more information about them. He finds brief biographies of each person on ChemGlobal's corporate Website, a profile of the CFO in Forbes Magazine, and an article in a local newspaper mentioning that the COO's son had recently graduated from Yale and had won a Rhodes Scholarship.

Bob also gets more information on a new methodology being used successfully in the pharmaceutical industry and, by asking questions in the discussion forum, finds that it would be easily transferable to ChemGlobal's situation. Bob also spends some time on the knowledge network taking a self-paced course on writing a winning proposal, even though he knows that the company will assign a principal and a proposal writer to work with him at the appropriate time. Using what he learns from the proposal writing course, he starts organizing the information he has gathered so far into a more usable form.

At Wednesday morning's meeting with Claire and Mary, Bob meets Dan Robertson, a local principal in the firm, and Bill Duplak from the bids and proposals group. Claire presents the work that Bob had done so far. Mary says that she has already talked with ChemGlobal's COO, Frank Chu, who gave her some more background on the cancelled project. Chu said that ChemGlobal would welcome a proposal from ProConsul Advisory Services if it can meet two conditions. First, ChemGlobal will have to meet the deadline of 18 months (given that the other consulting firm had already wasted six months) and second, it will have to come in within the $1.5 million that was left from the original budget. She reports that she has also set up a meeting with Chu and several of his staff members for the following Tuesday morning to get more background and make a very general presentation on ProConsul Advisory Services' capabilities in this area of practice.

Bob is to work with Dan and Bill to get the presentation together. It is to be no more than 15 minutes and will be presented to Chem-Global by Mary. They plan to meet first thing Monday morning to review it.

Over the next several days, Bob, Dan, and Bill work to put the presentation together. They use tools on the knowledge network to brainstorm ideas, jointly develop an outline, and finally prepare a set of slides for the presentation. They call on libraries of background information (boilerplate material) for some of the presentation and modify several slides that they took from other presentations in the library. They also learn much from each other. Bob has the knowledge of the customer and the specific application areas to be targeted, based on his research and learning throughout the process. Dan has knowledge of ProConsul's approaches and business practices from his years in the firm. He also knows Mary's preferred presentation style from his several years of experience working with her. Bill has knowledge of past proposals and the resources of the proposal library and toolbox. After several iterations, they have the slides assembled and a set of notes for Mary by Friday noon. They send them to her by email so that she can review them over the weekend to prepare for the Monday morning session.

At the Monday review, Mary is very pleased with the work done by Bob, Dan, and Bill. She changes a few words to suit her language and style preferences and adds one slide with a quotation from her conversation with Frank Chu from ChemGlobal. By noon on Monday, the presentation is complete.

THE REST OF THE STORY

I'll stop the story here, except to say that the presentation went well, that a proposal team was formed to develop the formal proposal for ChemGlobal, and that ProConsul Advisory Services ended up with a $1.4 million contract covering a 12-month project. Winning Chem-Global's business was accomplished in record time because of the investment the company had made in ISDL and in developing its knowledge network.

As Bob proudly deposited his commission check for the sale, he reflected on how much he had learned in his first few months at ProConsul, and how the company's knowledge network had enabled and facilitated both his learning and his first big commission.

ProConsul's initial sales training was a one-week residential program at the firm's corporate-training center in Ohio. The training included an overview of the firm, its structure, its major lines of business, its customer base, and it work methods. Much time was dedicated to the use of the many learning resources available through the company's training group and the company's knowledge network. Of the five days spent in training, Bob spent two full days in the learning laboratory, where he learned how to use his PC and how to access and use the knowledge network and the many ISDL resources and tools that reside on that network.

Bob used several self-study programs from the learning-resources database to learn more about specific areas of company expertise and practice. This helped him formulate his plan for ChemGlobal and to match ChemGlobal's business needs to services that ProConsul could provide. Other self-study modules taught him about the general format used by ChemGlobal for writing proposals and for pricing its work.

The learning-resources database also provided him with the tools to do background research on ChemGlobal through financial and news databases, as well as indexes of magazines and journals. The news-service subscription will keep him up to date on the latest happenings at ChemGlobal as he continues to work to expand ProConsul's relationship and the scope of its business with ChemGlobal. Tools and templates on the knowledge network, as well as the library of boilerplate text, helped him put the package together in the approved format.

The content database helped him research the work previously done for ChemGlobal by the firm, as well as other proposals written by the firm. He was also able to learn about other ProConsul projects done in the chemical industry for ChemGlobal's competitors.

From Bob's point of view, the most useful feature of the knowledge network was the connections database. Bob had done this type of background research before and could do it again without the aid of the knowledge network, but he knew it required a much greater investment of his time. The knowledge network made finding the necessary information much faster. The connections database enabled him to find people throughout ProConsul's worldwide operations that he never would have been able to find on his own. In his previous job with another consulting firm, Bob had built a very good personal network of contacts throughout the firm, but it had taken him five years to do it. Here, he made better contacts within his first month.

ProConsul's knowledge network was remarkable. It contained masses of data, measured in hundreds of gigabytes of computer storage. The tools provided within the knowledge network made it easy for Bob to sort through all of that data and find the information—data that has relevance and purpose, according to the learning model— that he needed quickly and efficiently.

Bob also realized that the firm's knowledge network contained only explicit data. What became even more valuable in learning about

ChemGlobal and in winning its business was the tacit knowledge of many ProConsul employees scattered around the world. Although the connections database enabled Bob to find many of these people, the network's communications tools allowed him to engage in a dialogue with these people to draw out their tacit knowledge about ChemGlobal's business challenges, about people within ChemGlobal, and about ProConsul's experience with ChemGlobal, with other chemical companies, and about ProConsul's relevant experience in other industries.

Because he was able to immediately use that information on the ChemGlobal proposal, he immediately transformed it into his own personal knowledge. In essence, he became ProConsul's expert on ChemGlobal.

One more step remained that Bob had to take with respect to the knowledge network. In his initial sales training, the instructors told him how to use the knowledge network but also emphasized that he also had to contribute to it. So even as the contract with ChemGlobal was being signed, Bob signed back onto the knowledge network and, using tools provided there, made his contributions:

- He summarized the new contract with ChemGlobal and submitted it to the content database.
- He updated his own profile in the connections database to list his new contacts at ChemGlobal.
- He also submitted several articles uncovered during his research that he thought would make good resources for others working in the chemical industry.

Appropriate managers of the knowledge network would later review his submissions and edit them as necessary. They would be then incorporated into the various databases for use by other employees.

Finally, Bob made some notes in his personal journal about his experiences and his contributions to the success of this bid and, through his additions to the knowledge network, the firm's business in general. He would use these notes when it came time for his annual performance review.

EXPANDING THE STORY BEYOND BOB AND PROCONSUL

Is Bob's story unique to his chosen profession of sales or to ProConsul's consulting business? Although many companies' initial forays into knowledge management have revolved around their sales groups, and although consulting firms have generally been at the forefront of the knowledge management revolution, building a knowledge network can help virtually any company in any industry across all job functions. For example:

- Assembly workers in scattered plants can share innovations they have made locally and, when faced with a problem they can't seem to solve locally, seek the collective wisdom of their fellow workers from across the globe (or in the plant across town).

- A company's finance organization can share financial data and the latest tax laws and rulings with group controllers and finance staffs spread across many states and countries.

- Purchasing managers can share information on sources, quality, delivery time, and price with each other. For example, a purchasing manager in Argentina may have a local source for certain materials needed by the company's French operations.

- Country marketing managers can use the knowledge network to share their local marketing materials and to brainstorm electronically about how best to introduce the company's new service line simultaneously around the globe.

- Design-engineering teams can call on the best talent available, regardless of location, to form a team to design the company's next-generation product. Using the tools of the knowledge network, team members from several different countries can share their ideas and work as if they were located in contiguous offices.

- By publishing training materials in the learning-resources database, the company's training group can make those materials available to employees around the world simultaneously. If the materials need to be updated at some point in the future, the revisions can be made to the single copy in the database, so that everyone accessing the learning resources will always be getting the most current version.

- A company expert on a given topic can mentor many people simultaneously, regardless of location, by holding a network-based seminar and then hosting an ongoing discussion forum. By hosting the discussion forum, the expert can choose when he or she has time to answer questions, rather than being repeatedly disturbed by telephone calls and email messages.

Making ISDL and a knowledge network work is not an easy task. Although there are many technology-based products available in today's marketplace, and a dozen or more are announced every month, the technological choices are the easy part of the effort. With technology becoming ever less expensive, with corporate networks growing in scope and bandwidth, it will not take many more years before every employee has at his or her fingertips the technology to fully, quickly, and inexpensively use a knowledge network. Two-way, full-motion video at the desktop will be as commonplace in five years as email is today. Large computer-based training programs will be downloaded to the employee's desktop or home computer in seconds rather than an hour or more. Searches of large content databases will be made more intuitive and will be done in seconds. Face-to-face conferences will take place daily from employees' offices scattered around the world—all set up at the click of a mouse. Automated translation programs will enable people to communicate across language barriers.

The more difficult task is to create a positive learning environment, in which every employee is motivated to continuously learn and every employee is motivated to share his or her knowledge with others. Managers must learn how to manage differently, and leaders must take a more active role in leading these changes. It also requires a major shift on the part of the traditional training group to move beyond formal instructional design, development, and delivery to roles as learning facilitators and coaches.

Is it possible for your organization to realize the full benefits of the opportunities that independent, self-directed learning can offer to the company and to the individual employee? The answer is an emphatic yes, but only if the company and every employee are willing to experience the discomfort of change in exchange for future benefits. It is my hope that this book has provided you with some guidance and some practical ideas on how to make ISDL work in your own organization.

LEARNING ASSIGNMENT

Think back over the past three months. Make a list of all of the learning methods you have used and list them in the table below:

	WITHIN YOUR ORGANIZATION	OUTSIDE YOUR ORGANIZATION
FORMAL TRAINING/ LEARNING PROGRAMS		
INFORMAL LEARNING ACTIVITIES		
KNOWLEDGE-SHARING ACTIVITIES— FROM YOU TO OTHERS		
KNOWLEDGE-SHARING ACTIVITIES— FROM OTHERS TO YOU		

Using Bob's story in this chapter, as well as the many other examples contained in this book, answer the following questions:

- What other types of learning activities would have added value to your work?
- How could you have undertaken those learning activities?
- How can you improve your organization's learning capacity and the range of its individual and group-learning activities in the future?
- How can you begin planning for the future? Make a commitment to yourself and to your organization to get started today!

References

Brown, J.S. (1998). "Research That Reinvents the Corporation." In *Harvard Business Review on Knowledge Management.* Boston: Harvard Business School Press.

Brown, T. (1999). MG—The New Ideas Website. http://www.mgeneral.com/1-lines/98-lines/-022198li.htm.

Business Channel Website. (1999). http://www.pbsbusinesschannel.com.

Caudron, S. (1999, August). "Free Agent Learner." *Training & Development,* 28.

Douglass, J. (1999, May). "Marketing the CBT Program Internally." Presentation at Perspectives '99, a conference sponsored by CBT Systems. San Francisco.

Fuller, J. (1999). "Understanding Human Performance Improvement." In *Performance Interventions: Selecting, Implementing, and Evaluating the Results,* B. Sugrue & J. Fuller, editors. Alexandria, VA: American Society for Training & Development.

Fisher, K., and M.D. Fisher. (1999). "Think With a Distributed Mind." Management General Website. http://www.mgeneral.com/3-now/98-now/042598kf.htm.

Garvin, D.A. (1993, July–August). "Building a Learning Organization." *Harvard Business Review, 71*(4), 78–82.

International School of Information Management Website. (1999). http://www.isim.com.

Labarre, P. (1999, May). "How to Be a Real Leader." *Fast Company* 62.

Lamont, J. (1999). "Cost-Effective Computer-Based Training." *KM World Magazine* Website. http://www.kmworld.com/feature.articles/index_articles.cfm?content=online_training.

Learn2.com Website. (1999). http://www.learn2.com.

Manasco, B. (1999, April). "Managing Content and Connections." *Knowledge Inc.,* 4(4), 12.

Marshall, C., L. Prusak, and D. Shpilberg. (1996, Spring). "Financial Risk and the Need for Superior Knowledge Management." *California Management Review, 25,* 76.

Masie, E. (1999a, May 10). *Techlearn Trends, 121.* http://www.masie.com.

Masie, E. (1999b, May 24). *Techlearn Trends, 123.* http://www.masie.com.

McDermott, L. (1999). "Coach!" Management General Website. http://www.mgeneral.com/3-now/99-now/031099lm.html.

National Technological University Website. (1999). www.ntu.edu.

Pennsylvania State University. (1999). TRDEV-L listserv discussion group. http://train.ed.psu.edu/trdev-l.

Peters, T., and Waterman, R. (1988). *In Search of Excellence.* New York: Warner Books.

Purser, R.E. (1999). "Move to Self-Management!" Management General Website. http://www.mgeneral.com/3-now/99-now/051299rp.htm.

Quinn, J.B., P. Anderson, and S. Finkelstein. (1996, April). "Managing Professional Intellect." *Harvard Business Review, 74*(2), 71–81.

Tobin, D.R. (1997). *The Knowledge-Enabled Organization: Moving from Training to Learning to Meet Business Goals.* New York: AMACOM.

U.S. Distance Learning Association Webpage. (1999). http://usdla.org/Pages/define.html.

Additional Resources

LEARNING AND KNOWLEDGE IN THE WORKPLACE

Brown, J.S. (1999). *Seeing Differently: Insights on Innovation.* Boston: Harvard Business School Press. This is the latest book by John Seely Brown, a pioneer in the field of individual, group, and organizational learning.

Davenport, T., and L. Prusak (1997). *Working Knowledge: How Organizations Manage What They Know.* Boston: Harvard Business School Press. Tom Davenport and Lawrence Prusak are two of the leading authorities on knowledge management.

Drucker, P. (1999, Winter). "Knowledge-Worker Productivity: The Biggest Challenge." *California Management Review,* 79–94. Peter Drucker has led the revolution leading to the valuing of knowledge and the knowledge worker in industry.

Tobin, D.R. (1994). *Re-Educating the Corporation: Foundations for the Learning Organization.* New York: John Wiley & Sons.

Tobin, D.R. (1996). *Transformational Learning: Renewing Your Company Through Knowledge and Skills.* New York: John Wiley & Sons.

TECHNOLOGY-BASED TRAINING

Gayeski, D. (1997). *Designing and Managing Computer Mediated Instruction: An Interactive Toolkit.* Ithaca, NY: OmniCom Associates. Diane Gayeski provides a very good, very basic guide to CBT in this publication.

Hall, B. (1997). *Web-Based Training Cookbook.* New York: John Wiley & Sons. This book is one of my favorite on Web-based training.

Marx, R.J. (1999). *The ASTD Media Selection Tool for Workplace Learning.* Alexandria, VA: American Society for Training & Development. This resource is a particularly useful resource for selecting learning technologies.

Sanders, E. (1999). "Learning Technologies." *Info-line,* issue no. 9902. Ethan Sanders provides a basic guide to learning technologies in this article.

INDEPENDENT, SELF-DIRECTED LEARNING

Knowles, M.S. (1988). *Self-Directed Learning: A Guide for Learners and Teachers.* New York: Cambridge Book Company. No list of resources would be complete without a reference to Malcolm Knowles.

London, M., and J.W. Smither. (1999, Spring). "Empowering Self-Development and Continuous Learning." *Human Resource Management, 38*(1), 3–15. This article shows how organizations can encourage self-development.

Rothwell, W.J., editor. *The Sourcebook for Self-Directed Learning.* Amherst, MA: HRD Press. Check out this reference if you want to learn how to develop self-directed learning materials.

THE NEW TRAINER

Bachler, C.J. (1997, June). "The Trainer's Role is Turning Upside Down." *Workforce,* 93–105. What will the movement to independent, self-directed learning mean to the corporate trainer? See this article.

Furst-Bowe, J.A. (1996, October). "An Analysis of the Competencies Needed by Trainers to Use Computer-Based Technologies and Distance Learning Systems." *Performance Improvement Quarterly,* 57–78. For an inventory of the new skills that trainers will need with respect to technology-based training, see this article.

Sorohan, E.G. (1996, March). "The Performance Consultant at Work." *Training & Development,* 34–38. This article describes the movement over the past decade to move trainers into new roles as "performance consultants."

WEBSITES OF INTEREST

American Society for Training & Development Website. (http://www.astd.org). This Website always has interesting articles from its publications and a wealth of other information. Be certain to check out its extensive listing of links to other Websites of interest.

Corporate Learning Strategies Website. (http://www.tobincls.com). Dan Tobin's Website has information on his background, seminars, a number of articles, and information on his books.

International Society for Performance Improvement (ISPI) Website. (http://www.ispi.org). In the area of performance consulting, you should check out this organization's Website.

Masie Center's Website. (http://www.masie.com). This Website offers the latest news on technology-based training. You may also request a free subscription to Elliott Masie's email newsletter from this site.

MG—The New Ideas Website. (http://www.mgeneral.com). See this Website for the latest management, leadership, and learning ideas. It contains book reviews, interesting interviews, and essays by some of the today's leading thinkers.

TRDEV-L listserv. (http://kell167.ed.psu.edu/TRDEV-L/). David Passmore at Pennsylvania State University runs this discussion forum, which has more than 5,000 subscribers from around the world. To find out more about the listserv group and how to subscribe, visit the Website.

About the Author

Daniel R. Tobin is the dean of Getronics Virtual University (formerly Wang Global Virtual University). Getronics is a $4 billion network technology services and solutions company, with more than 30,000 employees working in 44 countries. He is also the president of Corporate Learning Strategies, an independent consulting organization. This organization is dedicated to helping HR and training organizations align their work more closely with their companies' strategic business directions and expand their repertoires from traditional training activities to a more encompassing model of employee and organizational learning.

He has written three books: *The Knowledge-Enabled Organization: Moving from Training to Learning to Meet Business Goals* (1997), *Transformational Learning: Renewing Your Company Through Knowledge and Skills* (1996), and *Re-Educating the Corporation: Foundations for the Learning Organization* (1994). His articles and press interviews have appeared in leading business publications on four continents.

Tobin has more than 25 years of experience in the training field, including more than a decade with Digital Equipment Corporation. He holds a master's degree from the Johnson Graduate School of Management at Cornell University and a doctorate in the economics of education from Cornell University. He is also an adjunct professor in the graduate management program of Emmanuel College in Boston, Massachusetts, where he teaches courses on leadership, teamwork, and organization development.

As any creator of an ISDL resource will tell you, Tobin can only gauge the success and usefulness of this resource by receiving feedback from you, the reader. Any comments can be addressed to him via email at DanielTobin@att.net.